Balanced Literacy

Through Cooperative Learning & Active Engagement

by Sharon Skidmore

Jill Graber

In consultation with Jackie Minor

Kagan

Kagan Publishing
981 Calle Amanecer
San Clemente, CA 92673
1 (800) 933-2667
www.KaganOnline.com

ISBN: 978-1-879097-96-4

Balanced Literacy
Third Grade

Introduction

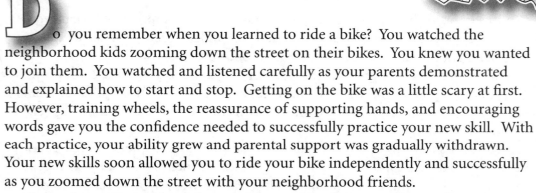

Do you remember when you learned to ride a bike? You watched the neighborhood kids zooming down the street on their bikes. You knew you wanted to join them. You watched and listened carefully as your parents demonstrated and explained how to start and stop. Getting on the bike was a little scary at first. However, training wheels, the reassurance of supporting hands, and encouraging words gave you the confidence needed to successfully practice your new skill. With each practice, your ability grew and parental support was gradually withdrawn. Your new skills soon allowed you to ride your bike independently and successfully as you zoomed down the street with your neighborhood friends.

Just as learning to ride a bike requires a series of supported steps, literacy requires guiding the learner through scaffolded instruction. The balanced literacy components provide the framework for developing deep thinkers and strategic readers. Balanced literacy increases teachers' effectiveness as they explicitly instruct through varying degrees of demonstration and practice, teacher feedback, and ongoing assessment.

[Effective teachers provide] just the right amount of support that allows the learner to assume increasing control of the task. It's a gentle dance that requires careful leading, following, and occasionally sidestepping. Gradually, as students become competent, we reduce the amount of support we offer. Intrinsic to this belief is allowing enough time, support, and feedback.

Regie Routman

Third Grade
Book Organization

In this book we have provided lessons and activities to support the balanced literacy components of aloud, shared, guided, and independent practice to strengthen national standards in comprehension, word study, vocabulary, fluency, and writing. Research emphasizes that learners need to acquire skills in these areas to be proficient readers and writers. Activities appropriate for third grade students have been developed for each of the four sections in this book, incorporating Kagan Cooperative Learning Structures.

As educators ourselves, we understand the limited time teachers have to develop student materials to support the literacy outcomes for their particular grade level. One of our goals for this book was to develop teacher-friendly materials. Therefore, you will find blackline masters (cards, spinners, cubes, and mats) designed to support the activities in each section. These are located directly behind the direction page for each cooperative learning structure. You may want to consider copying these pages onto cardstock, for durability. Blank templates have been included for some of the activities, giving you the flexibility to tailor activities to closely match specific literature or skills for your individual class.

The five national literacy standards of comprehension, word study, vocabulary, fluency, and writing are addressed in separate sections of this book, with the exception of vocabulary, which is included in both the Comprehension and Word Study sections.

Section 1: Comprehension

Section 2: Word Study

Section 3: Fluency

Section 4: Writing

Balanced Literacy • Third Grade • Skidmore & Graber
Kagan Publishing • 1 (800) 933-2667 • www.KaganOnline.com

Third Grade
A Note to the Reader

The ideas for this book are drawn from our combined experiences in the elementary classroom and as literacy coaches. As educators we are always striving to maximize learning and make every moment count as we endeavor to educate our students. It is our intention that this book will be a resource for you as you systematically think about literacy: What are the needs of my students? How can I best deliver instruction? What is the most effective use of instructional time?

When we combine balanced literacy and Kagan Cooperative Learning, our classroom practices become more purposeful and connected, resulting in increased student performance. We hope that this book will be a guide as you strive to improve instruction and enhance student learning.

A special thanks to Dr. Jacqueline Minor, our former Assistant Superintendent of Curriculum and Instruction and the present Director of Curriculum and Instruction for Kagan Professional Development, whose vision and knowledge continues to challenge us professionally. It has been with her involved guidance and encouragement that the ideas for the lessons and activities were organized for this book. Because of Jackie, this book has now become a reality.

Appreciations:

- **Illustrations:** Erin Kant
- **Graphic Designers and Layout Artists:**
  Alex Core
  Jennifer Duke
  Becky Herrington
- **Copyeditor:** Kim Fields
- **Publications Director:**
  Miguel Kagan

Third Grade
Table of Contents

Section 1
Comprehension

Comprehension Resources

Comprehension Activities and Lessons

Section 2
Word Study

Word Study Resources

Word Study Activities and Lessons

Third Grade
Table of Contents Continued

Balanced Literacy • Third Grade • Skidmore & Graber
Kagan Publishing • 1 (800) 933-2667 • www.KaganOnline.com

Section 3
Fluency

Fluency Resources

Fluency Activities

Section 4
Writing

Writing Resources

Writing Activities

Balanced Literacy

Comprehension

Word Study

Fluency

Writing

Comprehension

Comprehension

Comprehension research as reviewed by the National Reading Panel (NICHD, 2000), suggests that students learn best when teachers are explicit in their instruction. This is most effectively accomplished when teachers tell students what they are expected to do and model their own thinking processes for the students (aloud). As students are encouraged to ask questions, discuss possible answers, and apply other comprehension strategies, active engagement increases (shared, guided, and independent).

Comprehension provides the purpose for all reading. Proficient readers are aware of their own thinking processes, making conscious decisions to apply different comprehension strategies as they read (e.g., awareness of text organizational patterns [text types and structures], figurative language meanings, vocabulary clarification, and metacognition deepen comprehension).

Table of Comprehension Resources

Page(s)	Resources	Balanced Literacy				
		Aloud	Shared	Guided	Independent	Literature Circles
Metacognitive Awareness						
10	Metacognitive Awareness Descriptions					
13	Metacognitive Awareness Definitions	●	●	●	●	●
14	Metacognitive Awareness Posters	●	●	●	●	●
27	Metacognitive Awareness Student Bookmark	●	●	●	●	●
28	Metacognitive Awareness Student Tally Sheet	●	●	●	●	●
29	Metacognitive Awareness Student Page Response	●	●	●	●	●
30	Student Clarification Checklist	●	●	●	●	●
31	Metacognitive Awareness Student Rubric and Response	●	●	●	●	●
32	Metacognitive Awareness Lesson Planning Form (Shared Read Aloud)	●	●			

Table of Comprehension Resources (continued)

Page(s)	Resources	Balanced Literacy				
		Aloud	Shared	Guided	Independent	Literature Circles
33	Book List for Metacognitive Awareness Shared Read Alouds	●	●			

Text Types and Text Structures

Page(s)	Resources	Aloud	Shared	Guided	Independent	Literature Circles
35	Text Type and Text Structure Resource Descriptions					
37	Four Text Types— Text Type Resource Page	●	●	●	●	●
39	Text Structures— Text Structures Resource Page	●	●	●	●	●
40	Four Text Types and Five Text Structures— Resource Page	●	●	●	●	●

Figurative Language

Page(s)	Resources	Aloud	Shared	Guided	Independent	Literature Circles
41	Figurative Language Resource Descriptions					
42	Figurative Language Definitions	●	●	●	●	●
43	Figurative Language Student Record Sheets	●	●	●	●	●

Table of Comprehension Activities and Lessons

Page(s)	Activities/Lessons	Blacklines	Balanced Literacy				
			Aloud	Shared	Guided	Independent	Literature Circles
46	RoundRobin						
47	RoundTable						
47	RallyRobin						
46	Metacognitive Awareness Shared Read Aloud Comprehension Lesson	• Comprehension Lesson	●	●			
49	**Showdown Activity**						
50	Metacognitive Terms and Definitions	• Card Set 1 • Card Set 2		●	●		
53	Text Structures— Definitions, Signal Words, Graphic Organizers	• Card Set 1 • Card Set 2		●	●		
58	Text Structures and Paragraphs	• Card Set 1 • Card Set 2 • Answer Key		●	●		
62	**Quiz-Quiz-Trade Activity**						
63	Text Types— Definitions	• 4 pages of question/ answer cards			●		
67	Text Structures— Definitions and Graphic Organizers	• 4 pages of question/ answer cards			●		
71	Text Structure Passages	• 5 pages of question/ answer cards			●		
76	Cause-Effect	• 5 pages of question/ answer cards			●		
81	Text Features	• 4 pages of question/ answer cards			●		
85	Figurative Language—Similes, Metaphors	• 7 pages of question/ answer cards			●		
92	Figurative Language— Alliteration, Idiom, Onomatopoeia, Hyperbole, Metaphor, Simile	• 10 pages of question/ answer cards			●		

Table of Comprehension Activities and Lessons (continued)

Page(s)	Activities/Lessons	Blacklines	Balanced Literacy				
			Aloud	Shared	Guided	Independent	Literature Circles
102	Homophone Definitions	• 7 pages of question/ answer cards			●		
109	Homophone Sentences	• 8 pages of sentence cards			●		
117	**Fan-N-Pick Activity**						
119	Text Features	• Fan-N-Pick Mat 3 pages of cards		●	●		
122	Story Elements (Fiction)	• Fan-N-Pick Mat 2 pages of cards		●	●		
124	Previewing Before Reading (Nonfiction)	• Fan-N-Pick Mat 2 pages of cards		●	●		
126	**Talking Chips Activity**						
127	Comprehension Question Cube (Before Reading)	• Question Cube		●	●		●
128	Comprehension Question Cube (After Reading)	• Question Cube		●	●		●
129	Comprehension Question Cube (Reflection)	• Question Cube		●	●		●
130	Questioning Cube	• Question Cube		●	●		●
131	**RoundTable Consensus Activities**						
132	Vocabulary Spinner	• Spinner (Vocabulary) • 1 page of sentence cards • 1 page of blank sentence cards		●	●	●	●
136	Retelling (Fiction)	• Puzzle Pieces • Puzzle Mat		●	●	●	●
138	Retelling (Nonfiction)	• Puzzle Pieces • Puzzle Mat		●	●	●	●
140	Text Feature (Nonfiction)	• Puzzle Pieces • Puzzle Mat		●	●		

Table of Comprehension Activities and Lessons (continued)

Page(s)	Activities/Lessons	Blacklines	Balanced Literacy				
			Aloud	Shared	Guided	Independent	Literature Circles
142	**RallyTable and RallyCoach Activity**						
143	"Roach" Anticipation Guide	• Anticipation Guide Sample • Anticipation Guide Student Form	●	●	●	●	●
145	**Listen-Sketch-Draft Activity**						
146	Listen-Sketch-Draft	• Listen-Sketch-Draft Form • Example Page	●	●	●	●	●
148	**Timed Pair Share Activity**						
149	Prediction Mat	• Prediction Mat • Blank Story Element Cards • 2 Story Element Example Cards	●	●	●	●	●
153	**Jot Thoughts and Sorting Activity**						
154	Prediction and Sorting Mat (Before and After Reading Knowledge)	• Jot Thoughts Mat • Sorting Mat			●	●	●
156	**Traveling Heads Together Activities**						
157	Idioms	• 4 pages of idiom cards	●	●	●		
161	Fable Morals	• 2 pages of fable moral cards	●	●	●		
163	**RallyCoach Activity**						
164	Idioms	• Idiom Mat • 2 pages of cards			●		
167	**Team Line-Ups Activity**						
168	Sequencing Events	• Sentence strips			●		

Comprehension Resources

Metacognitive Awareness Comprehension

Resources/Materials Descriptions

How do we, as teachers, help our struggling readers improve their comprehension? We can show them how to build up their sight words, build their book list, and build time to practice reading. All of these activities are valuable but won't improve comprehension until we help students build a bridge . . . a bridge between their brains and the text.

Years of research have provided teachers with a list of comprehension strategies that good readers use while reading. Good readers are actively thinking while they read. They are aware when meaning has broken down, and they stop to fix the confusion. These strategies (Clarifying, Connecting, Deciding What Is Important, Evaluating, Inferring, Monitoring, Predicting, Prior Knowledge, Purpose Setting, Questioning, Responding Emotionally, Retelling/Summarizing, and Visualizing) become the thinking tools needed for bridge building.

Metacognitive awareness means that the reader is aware of his or her thinking during the reading of various types of texts. Through metacognitive awareness lessons, students learn to apply self-monitoring comprehension strategies. The components of balanced literacy become the avenue for the teaching and strengthening of these metacognitive comprehension strategies. Students are supported as they hear the teacher explain and use the strategies (aloud); observe the teacher use the strategies with text and participate at specific points (shared); practice the strategies with direct support and feedback (guided); and own the strategies through additional practice opportunities (independent).

Metacognitive Awareness Definitions (p. 13)

- The teacher should have the students read a text or passage and be aware of what they are thinking about or doing as they read. Have them make a list of their reading behaviors or the questions they ask themselves as they are reading.
- Hold a class discussion and make a student-generated list of different reading behaviors used. Use discussion questions such as "Why did you _____?" and "How did it help you while you were reading?"
- Distribute the **Metacognitive Definitions** list to each student and guide the discussion to help students make connections between their reading behaviors and the list of strategies. The **Metacognitive Awareness Definitions** list can be kept in reading notebooks or journals for students to refer to while reading.
- Now that students are aware that good readers think while reading, the teacher should model these strategies by stopping at various points during read aloud, explaining what she or he is thinking.
- Use this activity with different text types (narrative, expository, persuasive, and technical).

Metacognitive Awareness Posters (p. 14–26)

As the teacher reads aloud, one strategy poster can be displayed or referred to at a time, helping to focus the students' attention on that one strategy being modeled and explained. For convenience, the strategy posters can be three-hole punched at the top and then put into a notebook. The notebook will easily stand on a hard surface next to the teacher and she or he can flip to each individual Metacognitive Awareness poster as it is modeled and discussed.

Metacognitive Awareness Student Bookmark (p. 27)

During the learning phase of teaching students about metacognition, students should have a bookmark that sits beside their text book as they independently read. This not only reminds the students to use the strategies, but is also helps attach a strategy label to their thinking.

Metacognitive Awareness Student Tally Sheet (p. 28)

As the teacher reads aloud, students can tally each time that the teacher models a strategy. Students can also write notes, thoughts about the strategy, or specific questions that the teacher asked herself or himself aloud while reading. This activity will help the student identify the strategy that was used, attach a label to it, and think how it helped with comprehension.

Metacognitive Awareness Student Page Response (p. 29)

While reading and preparing for guided reading groups or literature circles, students can use the Metacognitive Awareness Student Page Response sheet to give page numbers and identify passages where they used comprehension strategies while reading. These recorded selections becomes discussion points as the students share their thinking with the group. The purpose of this activity is to help the students understand that readers use multiple strategies while reading and that each reader might use different strategies.

Student Clarification Checklist (p. 30)

Good readers have a repertoire of strategies to use while reading. The Student Clarification Checklist will remind the students of strategies to use when decoding a word, understanding the meaning of a word, or understanding an idea. The goal is not only to help students know the clarification strategies, but to realize when another strategy should be tried.

Metacognitive Awareness Student Rubric and Response (p. 31)

After students have observed repeated modeling of the use of metacognitive strategies during teacher read aloud and shared read aloud, the Metacognitive Awareness Student Rubric and Response page can be used to scaffold the students toward independent use of the strategies. The rubric gives the students specific feedback that is necessary for improvement.

Metacognitive Awareness Lesson Planning Form (Shared Read Aloud) (p. 32)

As the teacher continues to model the metacognitive awareness strategies, the Metacognitive Awareness Lesson Planning Form can be used to preplan specific, targeted comprehension strategies.

Book List for Metacognitive Awareness Shared Read Alouds (p. 33)

The book list is a resource for teacher read aloud, shared read aloud, or student literature circles that will focus on metacognitive awareness strategies.

Metacognitive Awareness Definitions

Clarifying	What words or ideas don't I understand?
Connecting	What does this remind me of? • text to self • text to text • text to world
Deciding What's Important	What is important, based on my goals?
Evaluating	What do I think about this text? How can I use this information?
Inferring	Why do things happen? What does this probably mean?
Monitoring	Which parts are confusing? What fix-up strategies could I use?
Predicting	What might happen next?
Prior Knowledge	What do I know about it?
Purpose Setting	Why did the author write this?
Questioning	What questions do I have?
Responding Emotionally	How does the character feel?
Retelling or Summarizing	What was this text about?
Visualizing	What pictures, smells, sounds, tastes, and touches come to my mind?

Connecting

What does this remind me of?

- Text to self
- Text to text
- Text to world

Deciding What is Important

What is important, based on my goals?

Evaluating

What do I think about this text? How can I use this information?

Monitoring

Which parts are confusing? What fix-up strategies could I use?

Prior Knowledge

What do I know about it?

Balanced Literacy • Third Grade • Skidmore & Graber
Kagan Publishing • 1 (800) 933-2667 • www.KaganOnline.com

Questioning

What questions do I have?

Responding Emotionally

How does the character feel?

Metacognitive Awareness

Clarifying

Connecting

Deciding What Is Important

Evaluating

Inferring

Monitoring

Predicting

Prior Knowledge

Purpose Setting

Questioning

Responding Emotionally

Retelling or Summarizing

Visualizing

Metacognitive Awareness

Clarifying

Connecting

Deciding What Is Important

Evaluating

Inferring

Monitoring

Predicting

Prior Knowledge

Purpose Setting

Questioning

Responding Emotionally

Retelling or Summarizing

Visualizing

Metacognitive Awareness
Student Tally Sheet

	Clarifying
	Connecting
	Deciding What Is Important
	Evaluating
	Inferring
	Monitoring
	Predicting
	Prior Knowledge
	Purpose Setting
	Questioning
	Responding Emotionally
	Retelling or Summarizing
	Visualizing

Balanced Literacy • Third Grade • Skidmore & Graber
Kagan Publishing • 1 (800) 933-2667 • www.KaganOnline.com

Metacognitive Awareness
Student Page Response

p. _____	p. _____	p. _____	**Clarifying**
p. _____	p. _____	p. _____	**Connecting**
p. _____	p. _____	p. _____	**Deciding What Is Important**
p. _____	p. _____	p. _____	**Evaluating**
p. _____	p. _____	p. _____	**Inferring**
p. _____	p. _____	p. _____	**Monitoring**
p. _____	p. _____	p. _____	**Predicting**
p. _____	p. _____	p. _____	**Prior Knowledge**
p. _____	p. _____	p. _____	**Purpose Setting**
p. _____	p. _____	p. _____	**Questioning**
p. _____	p. _____	p. _____	**Responding Emotionally**
p. _____	p. _____	p. _____	**Retelling or Summarizing**
p. _____	p. _____	p. _____	**Visualizing**

Student Clarification Checklist

Page #	Word/Phrases

I used these strategies to help me:
- say the word
- understand the word
- understand the idea

❏ I looked for word parts.

❏ I asked where I had seen the word before.

❏ I reread.

❏ I used picture clues.

❏ I used context clues and punctuation.

❏ I used text features.

❏ I used the glossary or dictionary.

❏ other _____

Student Clarification Checklist

Page #	Word/Phrases

I used these strategies to help me:
- say the word
- understand the word
- understand the idea

❏ I looked for word parts.

❏ I asked where I had seen the word before.

❏ I reread.

❏ I used picture clues.

❏ I used context clues and punctuation.

❏ I used text features.

❏ I used the glossary or dictionary.

❏ other _____

Metacognitive Awareness Student Rubric

Readers are actively thinking about their reading as they read.

	1	2	3	4
Metacognitive Awareness ❏ Clarifying ❏ Connecting ❏ Deciding What Is Important ❏ Evaluating ❏ Inferring ❏ Monitoring ❏ Predicting ❏ Prior Knowledge ❏ Purpose Setting ❏ Questioning ❏ Responding Emotionally ❏ Retelling or Summarizing ❏ Visualizing	• I wrote the strategy that I used while reading.	• I wrote the strategy that I used while reading. • My example of how I used the strategy was not clearly connected to the text.	• I wrote the strategy that I used while reading. • I gave at least one specific example from the text of when I used the strategy. • I explained how the strategy helped me as I read.	• I wrote several strategies that I used while reading. • I gave text support with explicit details of how I used the strategies. • I explained how the strategies helped me as I read.

Metacognitive Awareness Student Response

(Step 1): Name the strategy or strategies that you used while reading.

(Step 2): Text support: What were you reading about when you used the strategy or strategies?

(Step 3): How did the strategy or strategies help you as you read?

Metacognitive Awareness Lesson Planning Form

Shared Read Aloud

The teacher thinks aloud as she reads to the students. Overhead transparencies of specific pages from the book are used several times. Students participate by reading from the transparencies and then discussing the use of metacognitive strategies in teams.

Directions: Use this page to plan your lesson.

_____

by: _____

Page	Reading Materials	Metacognitive Strategies (Teacher Think Aloud)

Balanced Literacy • Third Grade • Skidmore & Graber
Kagan Publishing • 1 (800) 933-2667 • www.KaganOnline.com

Metacognitive Awareness Shared Read Alouds

Book Title	Author
America's Champion Swimmer	Adler, David A.
The Babe and I	Adler, David A.
Lou Gehrig, The Luckiest Man	Adler, David A.
Mama Played Baseball	Adler, David A.
Dandelions	Bunting, Eve
Fly Away Home	Bunting, Eve
Going Home	Bunting, Eve
Train to Somewhere	Bunting, Eve
Home Run: The Story of Babe Ruth	Burleigh, Robert
The Quiltmaker's Gift	Brumbeau, Jeff
Verdi	Cannon, Janell
The Great Kapok Tree	Cherry, Lynne
Miss Rumphius	Cooney, Barbara
Players in Pigtails	Corey, Shana
The Bat Boy and His Violin	Curtis, Gavin
Sam Johnson and the Blue Ribbon Quilt	Ernst, Lisa Campbell
My Brother Martin: A Sister Remembers Growing Up With the Rev. Dr. Martin Luther King Jr.	Farris, Christine King
The Patchwork Quilt	Flournoy, Valerie
Teammates	Golenbock, Peter
Luka's Quilt	Guback, Georgia
Sweet Clara and the Freedom Quilt	Hopkinson, Deborah
The Log Cabin Quilt	Howard, Ellen
The Boy and the Cloth of Dreams	Koralek, Jenny
Harvesting Hope: The Story of Cesar Chavez	Krull, Kathleen
Wilma Unlimited	Krull, Kathleen
The Rag Coat	Mills, Lauren
Uncle Jed's Barbershop	Mitchell, Margaree King
The Drinking Gourd: A Story of the Underground Railroad	Monjo, F. N.
Lighthouse: A Story of Remembrance	Munsch, Robert
Almost to Freedom	Nelson, Vaunda Micheaux

Metacognitive Awareness Shared Read Alouds (continued)

Book Title	Author
The Keeping Quilt	Polacco, Patricia
Mrs. Katz and Tush	Polacco, Patricia
My Rotten Red-Headed Older Brother	Polacco, Patricia
Pink and Say	Polacco, Patricia
Thank You, Mr. Falker	Polacco, Patricia
Tar Beach	Ringgold, Faith
The Relatives Came	Rylant, Cynthia
When I Was Young in the Mountains	Rylant, Cynthia
Grandfather's Journey	Say, Allen
Amazing Animal Disguises	Sowler, Sandie
The Tenth Good Thing About Barney	Viorst, Judith
Follow the Drinking Gourd	Winter, Jeanette
Owl Moon	Yolen, Jane

Text Type and Text Structure Resource Descriptions

Awareness of Text Types and Text Structures Benefits Readers' Comprehension.

Text Types	Purpose	Text Structures
Narrative	to entertain	Sequence
Expository	to inform	Problem and Solution
Technical	to tell how to...	Compare and Contrast
Persuasive	to persuade	Description
		Cause and Effect

There are four general reasons why authors write. These are identified as text types. Identifying the text type of a passage lets the reader know what the author's goal was for writing the text. This knowledge allows the reader to set a purpose for reading.

Text structures are the organizational patterns found within the text types, which alert the reader to the arrangement of the text. Being aware of these structures and being able to identify them makes the text easier to understand. An author often chooses one main text structure for a piece, but may incorporate several of the structures throughout the writing.

The following text type and text structure resources are for teacher and student use as instruction is scaffolded. The cooperative learning structures, Showdown and Quiz-Quiz-Trade, located in this section of the book provide practice in identifying definitions, graphic organizers, and specific text examples for text types and text structures.

Four Text Types (p. 37)

These two pages, listing general characteristics of the four text types and examples of each, are resources for the teacher and students. The teacher and the students may want to collect authentic examples for each of these four categories as they are introduced.

Text Structures (p. 39)

Signal words are frequently used by authors, which give hints about the text structure used in the writing. This chart lists some of those words, as well as a brief description of the text structures.

Four Text Types and Five Text Structures (p. 40)

This chart was designed as a resource, allowing students to visualize both basic text type and text structure information. As students learn to identify the text structure(s) used in a text, a graphic organizer matching the organizational structure becomes a tool for increasing comprehension. The graphic organizers included here are basic examples; students should be encouraged to experiment with the use of additional graphic organizers.

Four Text Types

Text Type	Characteristics	Examples	
Narrative	• Entertains the reader • Tells a story • Contains character(s) and a setting • Contains events • Has a problem/resolution • Contains theme that explains meaning of story • May be written in first, second, or third person • Makes sense when read from beginning to end	• Biographies • Drama • Diaries • Fables • Fantasies • Folk tales • Historical fiction • Legends • Mysteries	• Myths • Novels • Personal narratives • Plays • Poetry • Science fiction • Short stories • Tall tales, etc.
Expository	• Informs the reader • Contains facts and information • Explains, describes, discusses • May compare and contrast or present problem and solution • Includes text features such as headings, subheadings, bolded words, charts, graphs, diagrams, captions, indexes, glossaries, table of contents, etc.	• ABC books • Autobiographies • Biographies • Book reports • Brochures • Cartoons • Catalogs • Comics • Definitions • Essays	• Interviews • Invitations • Journals • Lists • Magazine articles • Newspaper • Recounts of an event • Research papers • Speeches, etc.

Four Text Types

Text Types Resource Page (continued)

Text Type	Characteristics	Examples
Technical	• Nonfiction text • Gives information used to perform a task • May include explicit steps or graphics to show steps • Shortened or fragmented sentences • Numbered or bulleted lists • Organized in logical, orderly way • Focused on identified topic • Uses specific vocabulary terms • Balance of white space and text	• Brochures • Classified ads • Consumer information • Directions • Floor plans • Forms • Graphs and charts • How-to guides • Instructions • Job preparation manuals • Maps • Menus • Questionnaires • Recipes • Regulations • Schedules • School forms • Syllabi • Transcripts • Warranties, etc.
Persuasive	• Nonfiction • Author intends to convince reader to take a particular opinion or perform a certain action • Attempts to solve problem through change • Uses appeal to reason, emotional appeal, or endorsement by an influential figure (bandwagon approach, glittering gereralities, testimonials, citing authority, statistics)	• Advertisements • Book reviews • Brochures • Business letters • Charitable campaign appeals • Commercials • Debates (written) • Editorials • Essays • Letters to the editor • Movie critiques • Political campaign literature • Position papers • Posters • Speeches, etc.

Text Structures

Text Structures Resource Page

Text Type	Tells...	Signal Words		
Sequence	series or steps	• first • second • third • next	• finally • then • before • after	• now • during • while • not long after
Description	attributes, facts, and details about something	• some characteristics are • for instance	• in fact • in addition • for example • has a	• about • is • does
Compare and Contrast	similarities and differences	• different from • like • same as • similar to	• resembles • both • also • too	• more than • however
Cause and Effect	reasons why something happens or exists	• so that • because of • as a result of • since	• so • for this reason • in order to	• therefore • if...then
Problem and Solution	problem, attempted solutions, and results	• problem is • solution is • have solved this problem by		

Four Text Types

Text Type & Text Structures Resource Page

The four text types describe four general types of writing. Identifying the text type of a passage helps the reader set the purpose for reading and alerts the reader to the organization of the piece.

Narrative	Expository	Technical	Persuasive
• Entertains • Tells a story • Character(s), setting, problem, resolution	• Facts/ information • Text features (headings, bold words, charts, graphs, captions)	• Information to perform a task • Steps	• Author tries to convince reader to take a certain opinion or perform a certain action

Five Text Structures

Text structures are organizational patterns found within the text types. An author often chooses one main text structure for a piece but may incorporate several of the text structures throughout the piece.

Sequence	Problem and Solution	Compare and Contrast	Description	Cause and Effect
• Steps • Specific order	• Problem, which is solved	• Comparing how things are the same/ different	• Details	• Something causes something else to happen

Sequence:
1.
2.
3.
4.
5.

Problem and Solution:
Problem
Event
Event
Event
Solution

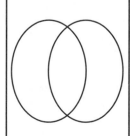

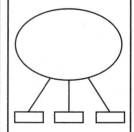

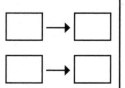

Balanced Literacy • Third Grade • Skidmore & Graber
Kagan Publishing • 1 (800) 933-2667 • www.KaganOnline.com

Figurative Language Resource Descriptions

Figurative language uses words in ways different from their literal meanings, to add interest and appeal to the senses. Figurative language is a tool that authors use to help readers visualize what is happening. The following resources can be used to help students identify various types of figurative language in their reading and attach a label to them. As students become familiar with the various types of figurative language, why the author chose to use it, and the affect it has on the reader, they will gain more confidence in their writing abilities and use of alliteration, analogies, hyperboles, idioms, metaphors, onomatopoeia, personification, and similes.

Figurative Language Definitions (p. 42)
Six different figurative language techniques are identified and defined on this chart. In addition, an example of each is provided. This chart is designed to be used as a teacher and student resource.

Figurative Language Student Record Sheets (p. 43–44)
This resource is used by students as they read independently, with partners, or in guided reading groups. Students record the figurative language they identify in their reading under the appropriate heading. Recording the page number provides opportunities to revisit the location of the figurative language in the text. Two different forms are included. The first guides students as they identify similes, metaphors, and idioms. The second adds alliteration, hyperboles, and onomatopoeia. These pages may be used for one text selection, or they may be used to keep ongoing records of identified figurative language over a period of time.

Figurative Language Definitions

Figurative Language Term	Definition	Example
Alliteration	The repetition of the same letter at the beginning of two or more words	Nine new nickels are needed now.
Hyperbole	An exaggeration	I'm so hungry, I could eat a bear.
Idiom	A familiar phrase that means something other than what it literally says	It's raining cats and dogs.
Metaphor	States that one thing is something else; is a comparison, but does not use the word *like* or *as*	My hands are icicles.
Onomatopoeia (on-o-mat-o-PEE-a)	A word that sounds like what it is describing; a sound effect	Murmur, creak, drip, pop, zip, wheeze
Simile	A comparison using the word *like* or *as*	The milk was as white as snow.

Balanced Literacy • Third Grade • Skidmore & Graber
Kagan Publishing • 1 (800) 933-2667 • www.KaganOnline.com

Figurative Language Student Record Sheets
(Simile, Metaphor, Idiom)

| Your Name: |
| Title of Text: |

Page	Example of Figurative Language
Simile	
Metaphor	
Idiom	

| Your Name: |
| Title of Text: |

Page	Example of Figurative Language
Simile	
Metaphor	
Idiom	

Figurative Language Student Record Sheets (continued)
(Alliteration, Idiom, Onomatopoeia, Hyperbole, Metaphor, Simile)

Your Name: _____

Title of Text: _____

Page	Example of Figurative Language	Page	Example of Figurative Language
Alliteration		**Hyperbole**	
Idiom		**Metaphor**	
Onomatopoeia		**Simile**	

Balanced Literacy • Third Grade • Skidmore & Graber
Kagan Publishing • 1 (800) 933-2667 • www.KaganOnline.com

Comprehension Activities and Lessons

Metacognitive Awareness Shared Read Aloud

Wilma Unlimited

How Wilma Rudolph Became the World's Fastest Woman by Kathleen Krull

The teacher thinks aloud as she reads to the students. Overhead transparencies of specific pages from the book are used several times. Students participate by reading from the transparencies and then discussing the use of metacognitive strategies in teams.

Text Page	Reading Materials	Metacognitive Strategies Teacher Think Aloud
1	**Read Aloud**	Discuss how the first sentence draws the reader in and makes one want to continue reading. **Connecting** (Text to Self): busy mom **Clarifying**: "home-remedies"
3	**Read Aloud**	Confirm or adjust definition of "home remedies" (mother took care of her at home).
5	**Shared Reading** *overhead transparency of text*	Students follow along as the teacher reads or the teams read together. **Predicting**: (after the second paragraph) *What might be wrong with Wilma's leg?* **Deciding What Is Important**: After the page is read, teams discuss what is important to remember. (Wilma has polio and will never walk again.)
7	**Read Aloud** *Metacognitive Awareness Student Rubric and Response (p. 31)*	**Rubric Writing** Model the writing of the use of a strategy for the students to observe using the rubric page. Example: **Understanding Character's Feelings**: *(Mom was busy, medical help was far away. She loved Wilma and she was determined to get her help even though she had many obstacles to overcome.)*
9	**Read Aloud**	**RoundRobin** In teams, students take turns responding orally to what rubric score they would give the modeled writing.
		Predict how Wilma might "fight back-somehow." **Deciding What Is Important**: Discuss what is important to remember.

Metacognitive Awareness Shared Read Aloud (continued)

Wilma Unlimited

Text Page	Reading Materials	Metacognitive Strategies Teacher Think Aloud
11	**Read Aloud**	After reading, think aloud how you visualized: the "ball zoom(ing) through the rim of the bushel basket" or Wilma sitting on the sidelines, "twitchy with impatience."
13–17	**Read Aloud** *Metacognitive Awareness Student Rubric and Response (one per team) (p. 31)*	**Visualizing:** **RoundTable** (with coaching) In teams, students take turns generating written responses for visualizing on the rubric page for steps 1, 2, and 3. **RoundTable** **Rubric Rating Practice** (Teams take turns reading their written responses.) • The Metacognitive Awareness Student Rubric is visible on the overhead. • Team 1 reads their written metacognitive response. • The other teams discuss what rubric score to give the response and the reason(s) why. • The teacher leads a discussion on the scoring of the response. **RoundTable** **Understanding Character's Feelings:** Teams describe traits of Wilma (determined, brave, etc.) and then share with whole class.
19	**Read Aloud**	**Questioning:** Why was it important for Wilma to mail the brace to the hospital? **RallyRobin** In pairs, students take turns summarizing the text to this point by verbalizing the "important things to remember."

Lesson

Metacognitive Awareness
Shared Read Aloud (continued)
Wilma Unlimited

Page	Reading Materials	Metacognitive Strategies Teacher Think Aloud
21	Read Aloud	**Questioning**: How did Wilma learn to play basketball? **RoundRobin** Students take turns, responding orally in their teams. **Questioning**: The cover shows Wilma as a runner, yet here we are reading about her being a basketball player. Good readers are always asking themselves questions as they read. I want to know how Wilma becomes a basketball player?
23	**Shared Reading** *overhead transparency of text*	Students read the page in teams. **Deciding What Is Important**: What is important to remember? *Coach wants her for his track and field team. Now I see the answer to my question and understand how Wilma will become a runner.*
25	Read Aloud	**Predicting**: *I know from reading about Wilma that she is a very determined person. I know she must be very excited to be at the Olympic Games, so I will predict that she will overcome her obstacles and do her best in the races.*
27–32	**Read Aloud**	Teacher reads the text, as students listen.
33	**Shared Reading** *overhead transparency of text*	Teams read the first paragraph together. **RoundRobin** Teams Predict what they think will happen. Teams share their predictions with the class and give reasons to support their thinking. Teams continue reading the second paragraph and then confirm/adjust their predictions.
35	Read Aloud	Teacher or teams discuss Wilma's character traits, which helped her become the "world's fastest runner." **RoundRobin** **Deciding What Is Important**: Teams take turns putting together the most important things to remember to form a summary of the text.

Activity

Comprehension Showdown

Teams play Showdown to master metacognitive terms, text structure definitions, and label text structure paragraphs.

Activity Steps

STRUCTURE

Showdown

1. Each team receives a Team Set of cards and every student receives a Student Set of cards.

2. The Team Set is placed facedown in the middle of the team. Students hold their Student Set in their hands.

3. The teacher selects one student to be the Showdown Captain for the first round.

4. The Showdown Captain selects the top card from the middle and reads it aloud.

5. Working alone, students individually identify an answer from their card set.

6. When finished, teammates signal they are ready.

7. The Showdown Captain calls, "Showdown!"

8. Teammates show their answers at the same time.

9. The Showdown Captain leads checking.

10. If correct, the team celebrates. If not, the teammates coach, then celebrate.

11. The person to the left of the Showdown Captain becomes the Showdown Captain for the next round.

Blacklines

Metacognitive Terms & Definitions
Showdown (Team Set)

Instructions: Copy one set of cards for each team. Cut apart.

Metacognitive Terms & Definitions — Team Set

Figuring out words or ideas, that I don't understand

Metacognitive Terms & Definitions — Team Set

Deciding how to use the information I learned

Metacognitive Terms & Definitions — Team Set

Choosing the key idea(s), based on my goals for reading

Metacognitive Terms & Definitions — Team Set

Deciding what parts are confusing and what fix-up strategies to use

Metacognitive Terms & Definitions — Team Set

Using clues to figure out why something happened or what something means

Metacognitive Terms & Definitions — Team Set

Deciding what might happen next

Metacognitive Terms & Definitions — Team Set

Thinking what the text reminds me of

Metacognitive Terms & Definitions — Team Set

Deciding the reason I am reading the text

Balanced Literacy • Third Grade • Skidmore & Graber
Kagan Publishing • 1 (800) 933-2667 • www.KaganOnline.com

Metacognitive Terms & Definitions
Showdown (Team Set)

Instructions: Copy one set of cards for each team. Cut apart.

Metacognitive Terms & Definitions — Team Set
Thinking about how the character(s) feel

Metacognitive Terms & Definitions — Team Set
Deciding what the text was about

Metacognitive Terms & Definitions — Team Set
Thinking about the pictures, smells, sounds, tastes, and textures from the text

Metacognitive Terms & Definitions — Team Set
Deciding what new information I want to learn

Metacognitive Terms & Definitions — Team Set
Deciding what I already Know about the topicv

Metacognitive Terms & Definitions
Showdown (Student Set)

Instructions: Copy one set of cards for each student. Cut apart.

Terms & Definitions — Student Set

 Monitoring

Terms & Definitions — Student Set

 **Summarizing and Retelling**

Terms & Definitions — Student Set

 Inferring

Terms & Definitions — Student Set

 **Responding Emotionally**

Terms & Definitions — Student Set

 Evaluating

Terms & Definitions — Student Set

 Questioning

Terms & Definitions — Student Set

 Deciding What Is Important

Terms & Definitions — Student Set

 Purpose Setting

Terms & Definitions — Student Set

 **Connecting**

Terms & Definitions — Student Set

 Prior Knowledge

Terms & Definitions — Student Set

 Clarifying

Terms & Definitions — Student Set

 Predicting

Terms & Definitions — Student Set

 **Visualizing**

COMPREHENSION
BlackLine

Text Structures—Definitions, Signal Words, Graphic Organizers
Showdown (Team Set)

Instructions: Copy one set of cards for each team. Cut apart.

Text Structures—Definitions,
Signal Words, Graphic Organizers—Team Set

Which text structure is arranged in a **series** or in **steps**?

Text Structures—Definitions,
Signal Words, Graphic Organizers—Team Set

Which text structure tells **facts** and **details** about something?

Text Structures—Definitions,
Signal Words, Graphic Organizers—Team Set

Which text structure points out **similarities** and **differences**?

Text Structures—Definitions,
Signal Words, Graphic Organizers—Team Set

Which text structure tells **reasons why** something happened?

Text Structures—Definitions,
Signal Words, Graphic Organizers—Team Set

Which text structure tells about a **problem** and the **solution** or solutions?

Text Structures—Definitions,
Signal Words, Graphic Organizers—Team Set

Which text structure uses words such as **first, second, and third**?

Text Structures—Definitions, Signal Words, Graphic Organizers
Showdown (Team Set)

Instructions: Copy one set of cards for each team. Cut apart.

Text Structures—Definitions, Signal Words, Graphic Organizers—Team Set

Which text structure uses words such as for instance, in fact, in addition, or for example?

Text Structures—Definitions, Signal Words, Graphic Organizers—Team Set

Which text structure uses words such as because of, therefore, or since?

Text Structures—Definitions, Signal Words, Graphic Organizers—Team Set

Which text structure uses words such as have solved this problem by …?

Text Structures—Definitions, Signal Words, Graphic Organizers—Team Set

Which text structure compares things that are the same and things that are different?

Text Structures—Definitions, Signal Words, Graphic Organizers—Team Set

Which text structure uses words such as now, next, or finally?

Text Structures—Definitions, Signal Words, Graphic Organizers—Team Set

Which text structure uses words such as before, during, or after?

Text Structures—Definitions, Signal Words, Graphic Organizers
Showdown (Team Set)

Instructions: Copy one set of cards for each team. Cut apart.

Text Structures—Definitions, Signal Words, Graphic Organizers—Team Set

Which text structure might use a graphic organizer such as:

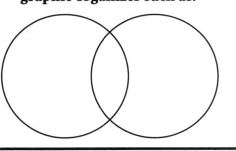

Text Structures—Definitions, Signal Words, Graphic Organizers—Team Set

Which text structure might use a graphic organizer such as:

| Problem |
| Event |
| Event |
| Event |
| Solution |

Text Structures—Definitions, Signal Words, Graphic Organizers—Team Set

Which text structure might use a graphic organizer such as:

Text Structures—Definitions, Signal Words, Graphic Organizers—Team Set

Which text structure might use a graphic organizer such as:

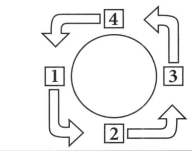

Text Structures—Definitions, Signal Words, Graphic Organizers—Team Set

Which text structure might use a graphic organizer such as:

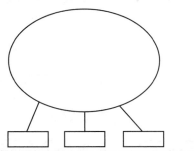

Text Structures—Definitions, Signal Words, Graphic Organizers—Team Set

Which text structure might use a graphic organizer such as:

Problem

Solution

Text Structures—Definitions, Signal Words, Graphic Organizers
Showdown (Team Set)

Instructions: Copy one set of cards for each team. Cut apart.

Text Structures—Definitions, Signal Words, Graphic Organizers—Team Set

Which text structure might use a graphic organizer such as:

Effect

Text Structures—Definitions, Signal Words, Graphic Organizers—Team Set

Which text structure might use a graphic organizer such as:

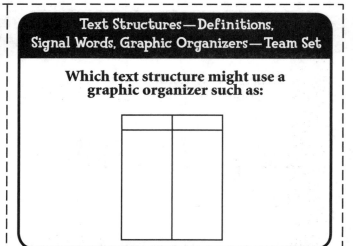

Text Structures—Definitions, Signal Words, Graphic Organizers—Team Set

Which text structure might use a graphic organizer such as:

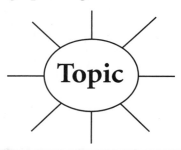
Topic

Text Structures—Definitions, Signal Words, Graphic Organizers—Team Set

Which text structure might use a graphic organizer such as:

If…	Then…	Because…

Text Structures—Definitions, Signal Words, Graphic Organizers—Team Set

Which text structure might use a graphic organizer such as:

1.
2.
3.
4.
5.

Text Structures—Definitions, Signal Words, Graphic Organizers—Team Set

Which text structure might use a graphic organizer such as:

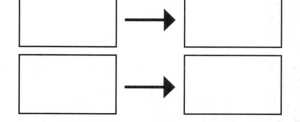

Text Structures—Definitions, Signal Words, Graphic Organizers
Showdown (Student Set)

Instructions: Copy one set of cards for each student. Cut apart.

Text Structures — Definitions, Signal Words, Graphic Organizers

Cause and Effect

Text Structures — Definitions, Signal Words, Graphic Organizers

Description

Text Structures — Definitions, Signal Words, Graphic Organizers

Compare and Contrast

Text Structures — Definitions, Signal Words, Graphic Organizers

Problem and Solution

Text Structures — Definitions, Signal Words, Graphic Organizers

Sequence

Text Structures and Paragraphs

Showdown (Team Set)

Instructions: Copy one set of cards for each team. Cut apart.

Text Structures and Paragraphs — Team Set

When ranchers in the Wild West wanted to keep their cattle from wandering away, they could not find enough timber or wood to make fences. They had a problem, and it was solved by L. B. Smith from Ohio in 1867. He invented barbed wire, which was made of sharp barbs on wood that were strung along a wire strand. Ranchers used this wire to make fences to keep their cattle on the ranches.

Text Structures and Paragraphs — Team Set

Because trees were scarce in the Wild West, ranchers did not have enough wood to make fences. Therefore, the cattle kept wandering away. In 1867, L.B. Smith invented barbed wire. Ranchers used this wire to make fences that would keep cattle on their ranches.

Text Structures and Paragraphs — Team Set

Barbed wire was a marvelous invention developed by L.B. Smith over 100 years ago. Small blocks of wood were spaced evenly on a long strand of steel wire. Sharp, pointy metal barbs stuck out of the blocks of wood.

Text Structures and Paragraphs
Showdown (Team Set)

Instructions: Copy one set of cards for each team. Cut apart.

Text Structures and Paragraphs — Team Set

It was difficult for ranchers to keep track of their cattle before the invention of barbed wire. But in 1867, when word spread about barbed wire, ranchers knew this was what they needed. First, the ranchers pounded 5-foot stakes into the ground around their property. Next, they wrapped the barbed wire around the first stake and the strung it to the next stake. Then, the wire was pulled tight before wrapping and securing it around the stake. They continued to do this around their property. After they finished with the wire, they made a gate for the opening. Finally, the ranchers could round up their cattle and corral them back onto their property. Safe at last!

Text Structures and Paragraphs — Team Set

Wooden fences and barbed wire have both been used to keep cattle on property. However, there are differences between wooden fences and barbed wire fences. Wooden fences were not always able to keep cattle from wandering away because trees were scarce and ranchers could not make the number of wooden fences they needed. On the other hand, when barbed wire fences were invented, ranchers from areas where wood was scarce used it to keep cattle from getting out.

Text Structures and Paragraphs
Showdown (Student Set)

Instructions: Copy one set of cards for each student. Cut apart.

Text Structures and Paragraphs—Student Set	Text Structures and Paragraphs—Student Set	Text Structures and Paragraphs—Student Set
Problem and Solution	**Cause and Effect**	**Description**

Text Structures and Paragraphs—Student Set	Text Structures and Paragraphs—Student Set
Sequence	**Compare and Contrast**

Text Structures and Paragraphs
Answer Key

Problem and Solution

When ranchers in the Wild West wanted to keep their cattle from wandering away, they could not find enough timber or wood to make fences. They had a problem, which was solved by L. B. Smith from Ohio in 1867. He invented barbed wire, which was made of sharp barbs on wood that were strung along a wire strand. Ranchers used this wire to make fences to keep their cattle on the ranches.

Description

Barbed wire was a marvelous invention developed by L.B. Smith over 100 years ago. Small blocks of wood were spaced evenly on a long strand of steel wire. Sharp, pointy metal barbs stuck out of the blocks of wood.

Cause and Effect

Because trees were scarce in the Wild West, ranchers did not have enough wood to make fences. Therefore, the cattle kept wandering away. In 1867, L.B. Smith invented barbed wire. Ranchers used this wire to make fences that would keep cattle on their ranches.

Sequence

It was difficult for ranchers to keep track of their cattle before the invention of barbed wire. But in 1867, when word spread about barbed wire, ranchers knew this was what they needed. First, the ranchers pounded 5-foot stakes into the ground around their property. Next, they wrapped the barbed wire around the first stake and the strung it to the next stake. Then, the wire was pulled tight before wrapping and securing it around the stake. They continued to do this around their property. After they finished with the wire, they made a gate for the opening. Finally, the ranchers could round up their cattle and corral them back onto their property. Safe at last!

Compare and Contrast

Wooden fences and barbed wire have both been used to keep cattle on property. However, there are differences between wooden fences and barbed wire fences. Wooden fences were not always able to keep cattle from wandering away because trees were scarce and ranchers could not make the number of wooden fences they needed. On the other hand, when barbed wire fences were invented, ranchers from areas where wood was scarce used it to keep cattle from getting out.

Activity

Comprehension Quizzes

Teams play Quiz-Quiz-Trade for repeated practice on text type, text structure, text features, figurative language, and homophones.

Activity Steps

1. Each student receives a card with a question on the front and an answer on the back.

2. Students stand up, put a hand up, and pair up with another student.

3. Partner A quizzes Partner B using the card.

4. Partner B answers the question.

5. Partner A praises if the answer is correct or provides the correct answer.

6. Partner B now quizzes Partner A, Partner A answers, and Partner B praises or provides the correct answer.

7. Partners trade cards and find a new partner to quiz. The activity continues for multiple rounds, allowing students to quiz and get quizzed multiple times.

STRUCTURE

Quiz-Quiz-Trade

Question (Front)   Answer (Back)

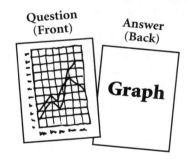

Graph

Variation

Mix-N-Match can be used on the activities with an asterisk (*) listed below. To do Mix-N-Match, at the end of Quiz-Quiz-Trade students rush to find partners with a card that matches theirs.

Blacklines

Text Types—Definitions
Quiz-Quiz-Trade

Instructions: Copy enough cards so each student has one card. Cut on dotted lines and fold in half.

Text Types—Definitions
Question

What text type **has a character(s), setting, problem, and solution?**

Text Types—Definitions
Answer

Narrative

Text Types—Definitions
Question

What text type **has text features** (headings, bold words, charts, graphs, captions, glossaries, etc.)?

Text Types—Definitions
Answer

Expository

Text Types—Definitions
Question

What text type **gives the steps needed to do something or make something?**

Text Types—Definitions
Answer

Technical

Text Types—Definitions
Question

What text type **gives reasons to perform a certain action?**

Text Types—Definitions
Answer

Persuasive

Text Types—Definitions
Quiz-Quiz-Trade

Instructions: Copy enough cards so each student has one card. Cut on dotted lines and fold in half.

Text Types—Definitions

Question

What text type **tells a story?**

Text Types—Definitions

Answer

Narrative

Text Types—Definitions

Question

What text type **gives facts and information?**

Text Types—Definitions

Answer

Expository

Text Types—Definitions

Question

What text type **gives information needed to perform a task?**

Text Types—Definitions

Answer

Technical

Text Types—Definitions

Question

What text type **tries to convince the reader?**

Text Types—Definitions

Answer

Persuasive

Text Types—Definitions
Quiz-Quiz-Trade

Instructions: Copy enough cards so each student has one card. Cut on dotted lines and fold in half.

Text Types—Definitions	Text Types—Definitions
Question What text type has a beginning, middle, and end?	**Answer** # Narrative
Question What text type **gives information that is true and can be proven (nonfiction)**?	**Answer** # Expository
Question What text type **often uses vocabulary specific to the topic and numbered/ bulleted lists?**	**Answer** # Technical
Question In what text type does the **author take an informed stand and gives reasons?**	**Answer** # Persuasive

Text Types—Definitions
Quiz-Quiz Trade

Instructions: Copy enough cards so each student has one card. Cut on dotted lines and fold in half.

Text Types—Definitions	Text Types—Definitions
Question What text type **makes sense when read from beginning to end?**	**Answer** **Narrative**
Question What text type **explains, describes, and discusses information?**	**Answer** **Expository**
Question What text type **often uses graphics to show steps?**	**Answer** **Technical**
Question What text type **sometimes uses emotional appeal to persuade the reader?**	**Answer** **Persuasive**

Text Structures—Definitions and Graphic Organizers
Quiz-Quiz-Trade

Instructions: Copy enough cards so each student has one card. Cut on dotted lines and fold in half.

Text Structures—Definitions & Graphic Organizers

Question

What text structure has **steps**?

Text Structures—Definitions & Graphic Organizers

Answer

Sequence

Text Structures—Definitions & Graphic Organizers

Question

What text structure has **a problem that is solved**?

Text Structures—Definitions & Graphic Organizers

Answer

Problem and Solution

Text Structures—Definitions & Graphic Organizers

Question

What text structure explains **how things are the same or different**?

Text Structures—Definitions & Graphic Organizers

Answer

Compare and Contrast

Text Structures—Definitions & Graphic Organizers

Question

What text structure has **details**?

Text Structures—Definitions & Graphic Organizers

Answer

Description

Text Structures—Definitions & Graphic Organizers

Question

What text structure tells how **something makes something else happen**?

Text Structures—Definitions & Graphic Organizers

Answer

Cause and Effect

Text Structures—Definitions and Graphic Organizers
Quiz-Quiz-Trade

Instructions: Copy enough cards so each student has one card. Cut on dotted lines and fold in half.

Text Structures—Definitions & Graphic Organizers

Question

What text structure is written in a specific time order?

Text Structures—Definitions & Graphic Organizers

Answer

Sequence

Text Structures—Definitions & Graphic Organizers

Question

What text structure has events that lead to figuring out the problem at the end?

Text Structures—Definitions & Graphic Organizers

Answer

Problem and Solution

Text Structures—Definitions & Graphic Organizers

Question

What text structure compares similarities and differences?

Text Structures—Definitions & Graphic Organizers

Answer

Compare and Contrast

Text Structures—Definitions & Graphic Organizers

Question

What text structure tells more about someone, something, or someplace?

Text Structures—Definitions & Graphic Organizers

Answer

Description

Text Structures—Definitions & Graphic Organizers

Question

What text structure explains how something occurred because of something else?

Text Structures—Definitions & Graphic Organizers

Answer

Cause and Effect

Text Structures—Definitions and Graphic Organizers
Quiz-Quiz-Trade

Instructions: Copy enough cards so each student has one card. Cut on dotted lines and fold in half.

Text Structures—Definitions & Graphic Organizers	Text Structures—Definitions & Graphic Organizers
Question — What text structure would use this graphic organizer? 1. 2. 3. 4. 5.	**Answer** # Sequence

Text Structures—Definitions & Graphic Organizers	Text Structures—Definitions & Graphic Organizers
Question — What text structure would use this graphic organizer? Problem Event Event Event Solution	**Answer** # Problem and Solution

Text Structures—Definitions & Graphic Organizers	Text Structures—Definitions & Graphic Organizers
Question — What text structure would use this graphic organizer?	**Answer** # Compare and Contrast

Text Structures—Definitions & Graphic Organizers	Text Structures—Definitions & Graphic Organizers
Question — What text structure would use this graphic organizer? 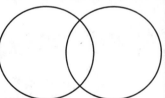	**Answer** # Description

Text Structures—Definitions & Graphic Organizers	Text Structures—Definitions & Graphic Organizers
Question — What text structure would use this graphic organizer? 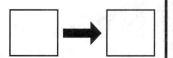	**Answer** # Cause and Effect

Text Structures—Definitions and Graphic Organizers
Quiz-Quiz-Trade

Instructions: Copy enough cards so each student has one card. Cut on dotted lines and fold in half.

Text Structures—Definitions & Graphic Organizers	Text Structures—Definitions & Graphic Organizers
Question What text structure would use this graphic organizer? 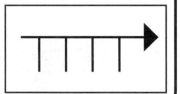	**Answer** # Sequence
Question What text structure would use this graphic organizer? 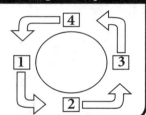	**Answer** # Sequence
Question What text structure would use this graphic organizer? 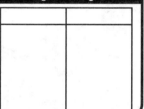	**Answer** # Compare and Contrast
Question What text structure would use this graphic organizer? 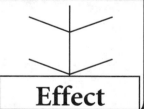	**Answer** # Cause and Effect
Question What text structure would use this graphic organizer? 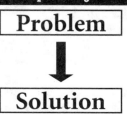	**Answer** # Problem and Solution

Text Structure Passages

Quiz-Quiz-Trade

Instructions: Copy enough cards so each student has one card. Cut on dotted lines and fold in half.

Text Structure Passages	Text Structure Passages
Question: What text structure is this passage? First we packed our suitcases. Then we piled into our little car. Before long we were on the way to grandma's house.	**Answer** **Sequence**
Question: What text structure is this passage? We didn't know how to get our cat down from the tree after the neighbor's dog chased her. The fire department came to the rescue.	**Answer** **Problem and Solution**
Question: What text structure is this passage? Tigers and lions are both cats. However, tigers have stripes and lions do not. Both have very good nighttime vision. Unlike lions, tigers like water and are good swimmers.	**Answer** **Compare and Contrast**
Question: What text structure is this passage? Butterflies are flying insects with two pairs of large, colorful, scaly wings. The wing scales overlap in rows. The color of the wings gradually fades.	**Answer** **Description**
Question: What text structure is this passage? We discovered that the batteries in our flashlight were dead when we tried to use it during the storm. Therefore, we were not able to see until the electricity came on.	**Answer** **Cause and Effect**

Text Structure Passages
Quiz-Quiz-Trade

Instructions: Copy enough cards so each student has one card. Cut on dotted lines and fold in half.

Text Structure Passages

Question: What text structure is this passage?

Before putting the model car together, we gathered our supplies. Then we were able to read and follow the directions. Before long our car was completed.

Text Structure Passages

Answer

Sequence

Text Structure Passages

Question: What text structure is this passage?

Mountain climbers get tired when climbing for many days. They need to sleep, but it is dangerous. Since they might roll off the edge, they sleep on ledges with ropes keeping them from falling off the mountain.

Text Structure Passages

Answer

Problem and Solution

Text Structure Passages

Question: What text structure is this passage?

Your lungs are like two balloons. When you take a breath, air rushes in, like when you blow up a balloon. When you breathe out, the air goes out and your lungs get smaller just like a balloon.

Text Structure Passages

Answer

Compare and Contrast

Text Structure Passages

Question: What text structure is this passage?

Cats are graceful. They have rounded faces, sandpapery tongues, and needle-like teeth. Cats are many different sizes. They have a variety of colors, fur length, eye colors, and voices.

Text Structure Passages

Answer

Description

Text Structure Passages

Question: What text structure is this passage?

The sun keeps Earth warm. If the sun did not shine on Earth, it would be so cold that no plants, animals, or people could survive. As a result of the sun, there is life on Earth.

Text Structure Passages

Answer

Cause and Effect

Text Structure Passages

Quiz-Quiz-Trade

Instructions: Copy enough cards so each student has one card. Cut on dotted lines and fold in half.

Text Structure Passages

Question: What text structure is this passage?

Sue lost her first tooth when she was five years old. Later, when she was six, she lost another tooth. Not long after, Sue lost two teeth in one day.

Text Structure Passages

Answer

Sequence

Text Structure Passages

Question: What text structure is this passage?

When an enemy tries to attack an armadillo, the armadillo has to plan. If the enemy gets too close, the armadillo rolls up into a hard ball. The hard, bony plates covering its body protect the armadillo.

Text Structure Passages

Answer

Problem and Solution

Text Structure Passages

Question: What text structure is this passage?

Hippos, walruses, and woodchucks all have large teeth. Hippos use their teeth to scare away enemies. Walruses use their teeth to pull themselves out of the water. Woodchucks use their teeth to chomp through tough plants.

Text Structure Passages

Answer

Compare and Contrast

Text Structure Passages

Question: What text structure is this passage?

Spiders force a liquid out through the spinnerets at the rear end of their bodies. The fluid hardens when it hits the air. The fluid makes silk. This silk may be thick or thin. It may also be sticky or dry. In addition, it may be smooth or bumpy.

Text Structure Passages

Answer

Description

Text Structure Passages

Question: What text structure is this passage?

Very tall trees grow in a tropical rain forest. Because the trees grow so close together, the leaves form a roof high above the ground, called a canopy, which blocks out the sky and the sun.

Text Structure Passages

Answer

Cause and Effect

Text Structure Passages
Quiz-Quiz-Trade

Instructions: Copy enough cards so each student has one card. Cut on dotted lines and fold in half.

Text Structure Passages

Question: What text structure is this passage?

Before you begin to bake chocolate chip cookies, remember to gather all of the ingredients. Next, turn on the oven to preheat it. Then, you are ready to begin measuring and mixing the dough.

Text Structure Passages

Answer

Sequence

Text Structure Passages

Question: What text structure is this passage?

It is dark as night in the deepest parts of the ocean. Most fish would find it very difficult or impossible to see, but the lantern fish has solved this problem. It carries its own flashlight.

Text Structure Passages

Answer

Problem and Solution

Text Structure Passages

Question: What text structure is this passage?

Eels are long and thin like snakes. Trying to hold onto an eel is like trying to hold onto a snake.

Text Structure Passages

Answer

Compare and Contrast

Text Structure Passages

Question: What text structure is this passage?

Lobsters are reddish-green and blue in color. They have two claws that can pinch. They also have eight legs. In addition, they have two antennae that help them feel to find out where they are.

Text Structure Passages

Answer

Description

Text Structure Passages

Question: What text structure is this passage?

Carol forgot to add yeast to the dough when she was baking. Therefore, her wheat bread did not rise, and she was not able to eat it.

Text Structure Passages

Answer

Cause and Effect

Text Structure Passages
Quiz-Quiz-Trade

Instructions: Copy enough cards so each student has one card. Cut on dotted lines and fold in half.

Text Structure Passages

Question: What text structure is this passage?

First, sharks use their keen sense of smell to track down an animal for lunch. Then they race toward the prey while steering with their tails. Finally, they open their mouths and bite hard!

Text Structure Passages

Answer

Sequence

Text Structure Passages

Question: What text structure is this passage?

If a starfish loses one of its arms in a fight, another one will soon grow in its place.

Text Structure Passages

Answer

Problem and Solution

Text Structure Passages

Question: What text structure is this passage?

Adult and baby langurs are quite different from each other in appearance. Adults have dark fur while babies are bright orange in color when they are born.

Text Structure Passages

Answer

Compare and Contrast

Text Structure Passages

Question: What text structure is this passage?

The shrill train whistle shrieked through the cold, icy night.

Text Structure Passages

Answer

Description

Text Structure Passages

Question: What text structure is this passage?

Because a plate of grapes were out in the hot sun, they turned into raisins within several days.

Text Structure Passages

Answer

Cause and Effect

Cause-Effect

Quiz-Quiz-Trade

Instructions: Copy enough cards so each student has one card. Cut on dotted lines and fold in half.

Cause-Effect **Question: Which is the cause? Which is the effect?** I left the bathtub water running to go answer the telephone. Water covered the bathroom floor.	**Cause-Effect** **Answer** **Cause:** I left the bathtub water running to go answer the telephone. **Effect:** Water covered the bathroom floor.
Cause-Effect **Question: Which is the cause? Which is the effect?** When I returned to my car, my purse was gone. I left my purse on the seat of my unlocked car while I quickly ran back into the store.	**Cause-Effect** **Answer** **Cause:** I left my purse on the seat of my unlocked car while I quickly ran back into the store. **Effect:** When I returned to my car, my purse was gone.
Cause-Effect **Question: Which is the cause? Which is the effect?** We had to bottlefeed two kittens. My cat had too many kittens to feed.	**Cause-Effect** **Answer** **Cause:** My cat had too many kittens to feed. **Effect:** We had to bottlefeed two kittens.
Cause-Effect **Question: Which is the cause? Which is the effect?** I meant to put gas in my car last night because it was on empty. I ran out of gas three blocks from my house.	**Cause-Effect** **Answer** **Cause:** I meant to put gas in my car last night because it was on empty. **Effect:** I ran out of gas three blocks from my house.
Cause-Effect **Question: Which is the cause? Which is the effect?** My alarm clock did not go off this morning. I was late for my ball game.	**Cause-Effect** **Answer** **Cause:** My alarm clock did not go off this morning. **Effect:** I was late for my ball game.

Cause-Effect

Quiz-Quiz-Trade

Instructions: Copy enough cards so each student has one card. Cut on dotted lines and fold in half.

Cause-Effect

Question: Which is the cause? Which is the effect?

John did not understand the math homework assignment.

John was daydreaming during math class.

Cause-Effect

Answer
Cause: John was daydreaming during math class.

Effect: John did not understand the math homework assignment.

Cause-Effect

Question: Which is the cause? Which is the effect?

The farmer left the gate open.

There were five sheep in the middle of the farmer's yard.

Cause-Effect

Answer
Cause: The farmer left the gate open.

Effect: There were five sheep in the middle of the farmer's yard.

Cause-Effect

Question: Which is the cause? Which is the effect?

I was so surprised that I jumped three feet high.

I walked into a dark room and everyone shouted, "Happy Birthday!"

Cause-Effect

Answer
Cause: I walked into a dark room and everyone shouted, "Happy Birthday!"

Effect: I was so surprised that I jumped three feet high.

Cause-Effect

Question: Which is the cause? Which is the effect?

It hasn't rained in two months.

The farmer is worried about the wheat he planted.

Cause-Effect

Answer
Cause: It hasn't rained in two months.

Effect: The farmer is worried about the wheat he planted.

Cause-Effect

Question: Which is the cause? Which is the effect?

A train stopped traffic for 25 minutes.

Tom was impatient as he sat in his car, waiting for the end of the train.

Cause-Effect

Answer
Cause: A train stopped traffic for 25 minutes.

Effect: Tom was impatient as he sat in his car, waiting for the end of the train.

Cause-Effect

Quiz-Quiz-Trade

Instructions: Copy enough cards so each student has one card. Cut on dotted lines and fold in half.

Cause-Effect

Question: Which is the cause? Which is the effect?

I have a horrible stomachache.

I had two pieces of cake, three hot dogs, and cotton candy at the school carnival.

Cause-Effect

Answer
Cause: I had two pieces of cake, three hot dogs, and cotton candy at the school carnival.

Effect: I have a horrible stomachache.

Cause-Effect

Question: Which is the cause? Which is the effect?

The paint turned green.

The artist poured the yellow paint into the blue paint.

Cause-Effect

Answer
Cause: The artist poured the yellow paint into the blue paint.

Effect: The paint turned green.

Cause-Effect

Question: Which is the cause? Which is the effect?

Rain came pouring down for three hours.

The sun came out and a beautiful rainbow appeared.

Cause-Effect

Answer
Cause: Rain came pouring down for three hours.

Effect: The sun came out and a beautiful rainbow appeared.

Cause-Effect

Question: Which is the cause? Which is the effect?

The gardener shoveled fertilizer around his plants.

The plants look so healthy and green now.

Cause-Effect

Answer
Cause: The gardener shoveled fertilizer around his plants.

Effect: The plants look so healthy and green now.

Cause-Effect

Question: Which is the cause? Which is the effect?

The bird stopped singing.

The man put a blanket over the birdcage.

Cause-Effect

Answer
Cause: The man put a blanket over the birdcage.

Effect: The bird stopped singing.

Cause-Effect
Quiz-Quiz-Trade

Instructions: Copy enough cards so each student has one card. Cut on dotted lines and fold in half.

Cause-Effect

Question: Which is the cause? Which is the effect?

I returned to the kitchen to find a milk puddle on the counter.

I left the carton of ice cream sitting on the counter.

Cause-Effect

Answer

Cause: I left the carton of ice cream sitting on the counter.

Effect: I returned to the kitchen to find a milk puddle on the counter.

Cause-Effect

Question: Which is the cause? Which is the effect?

Jill stayed in at recess so her teacher could help her with her math problems.

Jill was thrilled that she passed her math test today.

Cause-Effect

Answer

Cause: Jill stayed in at recess so her teacher could help her with her math problems.

Effect: Jill was thrilled that she passed her math test today.

Cause-Effect

Question: Which is the cause? Which is the effect?

There are holes in everybody's socks.

Rachel's new puppy will chew on anything it can sink its teeth into.

Cause-Effect

Answer

Cause: Rachel's new puppy will chew on anything it can sink its teeth into.

Effect: There are holes in everybody's socks.

Cause-Effect

Question: Which is the cause? Which is the effect?

The plant turned brown.

The plant was left in the dark closet for one month.

Cause-Effect

Answer

Cause: The plant was left in the dark closet for one month.

Effect: The plant turned brown.

Cause-Effect

Question: Which is the cause? Which is the effect?

I left my game pieces lying on the floor.

My game pieces were no longer on the floor after my mom vacuumed the carpet.

Cause-Effect

Answer

Cause: I left my game pieces lying on the floor.

Effect: My game pieces were no longer on the floor after my mom vacuumed the carpet.

Cause-Effect

Quiz-Quiz-Trade

Instructions: Copy enough cards so each student has one card. Cut on dotted lines and fold in half.

Cause-Effect

Question: Which is the cause? Which is the effect?

I left my window open today.

Two birds flew into my room.

Cause-Effect

Answer
Cause: I left my window open today.

Effect: Two birds flew into my room.

Cause-Effect

Question: Which is the cause? Which is the effect?

My arms and neck are red and sunburned.

It was sunny and warm outside yesterday, so I planted my vegetable garden.

Cause-Effect

Answer
Cause: It was sunny and warm outside yesterday, so I planted my vegetable garden.

Effect: My arms and neck are red and sunburned.

Cause-Effect

Question: Which is the cause? Which is the effect?

My friend and I are both covered with poison ivy.

My friend and I went on a walk in the woods looking for insects.

Cause-Effect

Answer
Cause: My friend and I went on a walk in the woods looking for insects.

Effect: My friend and I are both covered with poison ivy.

Cause-Effect

Question: Which is the cause? Which is the effect?

My sister watched a scary movie on TV last night.

My sister crawled in bed with me during the night because she didn't want to sleep alone.

Cause-Effect

Answer
Cause: My sister watched a scary movie on TV last night.

Effect: My sister crawled in bed with me during the night because she didn't want to sleep alone.

Cause-Effect

Question: Which is the cause? Which is the effect?

The marathon runner won the race in record time.

The marathon runner has been practicing for the race for months.

Cause-Effect

Answer
Cause: The marathon runner has been practicing for the race for months.

Effect: The marathon runner won the race in record time.

Text Features
Quiz-Quiz-Trade

Instructions: Copy enough cards so each student has one card. Cut on dotted lines and fold in half.

Text Features

Question: What text feature is this example?

- Little Dipper
- Big Dipper
- Orion, the Hunter
- Taurus

Text Features

Answer

Bullets

Text Features

Question: What text feature is this example?

Comets have orbits.

↑

Text Features

Answer

Bolded Word

Text Features

Question: What text feature is this example?

Text Features

Answer

Map

Text Features

Question: What text feature is this example?

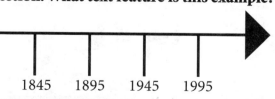

1845   1895   1945   1995

Text Features

Answer

Timeline

Text Features

Question: What text feature is this example?

| Meteors that fall to Earth are called meteorites. |

Text Features

Answer

Boxed Item

Text Features
Quiz-Quiz-Trade

Instructions: Copy enough cards so each student has one card. Cut on dotted lines and fold in half.

Text Features
Question: What text feature is this example?

New Students at School

	1st Grade	2nd Grade	3rd Grade	4th Grade
2003	4	3	1	0
2004	2	1	5	2

Text Features
Answer

Chart

Text Features
Question: What text feature is this example?

Text Features
Answer

Graph

Text Features
Question: What text feature is this example?

soft fur — ears — eyes — whiskers — claws — tail

Text Features
Answer

Diagram

Text Features
Question: What text feature is this example?

```
arachnid......... 8
eggs ................ 2, 17, 23
fly .................. 12
moth ............. 25
wasp .............. 4, 16
```

Text Features
Answer

Index

Text Features
Question: What text feature is this example?

Colorful insects are usually poisonous or bad–tasting.

Text Features
Answer

Caption

Text Features
Quiz-Quiz-Trade

Instructions: Copy enough cards so each student has one card. Cut on dotted lines and fold in half.

Text Features	Text Features
Question: What text feature is this example?	**Answer**
Polar bears dig their *dens* in snow or ice.	**Italicized Word**

Text Features	Text Features
Question: What text feature is this example?	**Answer**
Fun Fact Polar bears have large, flat paws, which help them walk on the snow. ← Page 34	**Sidebar**

Text Features	Text Features
Question: What text feature is this example?	**Answer**
	**Photograph**

Text Features	Text Features
Question: What text feature is this example?	**Answer**
The silk **dragline** will help save a spider from a serious fall.	**Colored Word**

Text Features	Text Features
Question: What text feature is this example?	**Answer**
Egyptians used beetle designs, called **scarabs**, in jewelry and paintings. ↑	**Stylized Word**

Text Features
Quiz-Quiz-Trade

Instructions: Copy enough cards so each student has one card. Cut on dotted lines and fold in half.

Text Features	Text Features
Question: What text feature is this example?	**Answer**
Bullfrog..2 Tree Frog..6 Poison Dart Frog..............................8 Horned Frog...................................10	# Table of Contents

Text Features	Text Features
Question: What text feature is this example?	**Answer**
Look Out Below!	# Heading

Text Features	Text Features
Question: What text feature is this example?	**Answer**
Adobe—Sun-dried brick of clay and straw **Bedouins**—Nomadic tribes **Desert**—A very dry land region **Irrigation**—Watering the land	# Glossary

Text Features	Text Features
Question: What text feature is this example?	**Answer**
 Bee 	# Label

Text Features	Text Features
Question: What text feature is this example?	**Answer**
Polar Bears ← by John Carter	# Title

Figurative Language
Similes, Metaphors
Quiz-Quiz-Trade

Instructions: Copy enough cards so each student has one card. Cut on dotted lines and fold in half.

Figurative Language—Similes, Metaphors

Question

Her eyes flashed like lightning.

This is an example of:
    a) simile
    b) metaphor

Figurative Language—Similes, Metaphors

Answer

Her eyes flashed like lightning.

a) simile

Figurative Language—Similes, Metaphors

Question

My mouth was a dry desert.

This is an example of:
    a) simile
    b) metaphor

Figurative Language—Similes, Metaphors

Answer

My mouth was a dry desert.

b) metaphor

Figurative Language—Similes, Metaphors

Question

Mrs. Hoops' nose was curved like the beak of a hawk.

This is an example of:
    a) simile
    b) metaphor

Figurative Language—Similes, Metaphors

Answer

Mrs. Hoops' nose was curved like the beak of a hawk.

a) simile

Figurative Language—Similes, Metaphors

Question

The trees in the forest were tall statues.

This is an example of:
    a) simile
    b) metaphor

Figurative Language—Similes, Metaphors

Answer

The trees in the forest were tall statues.

b) metaphor

Figurative Language
Similes, Metaphors
Quiz-Quiz-Trade

Instructions: Copy enough cards so each student has one card. Cut on dotted lines and fold in half.

Figurative Language—Similes, Metaphors

Question

The path was worn smooth as stone.

This is an example of:
- a) simile
- b) metaphor

Figurative Language—Similes, Metaphors

Answer
The path was worn smooth as stone.

a) simile

Figurative Language—Similes, Metaphors

Question

The ocean of wheat rippled in the distance.

This is an example of:
- a) simile
- b) metaphor

Figurative Language—Similes, Metaphors

Answer
The ocean of wheat rippled in the distance.

b) metaphor

Figurative Language—Similes, Metaphors

Question

The rocks in the desert stood like enormous sculptures.

This is an example of:
- a) simile
- b) metaphor

Figurative Language—Similes, Metaphors

Answer
The rocks in the desert stood like enormous sculptures.

a) simile

Figurative Language—Similes, Metaphors

Question

The book was a passport to adventure.

This is an example of:
- a) simile
- b) metaphor

Figurative Language—Similes, Metaphors

Answer
The book was a passport to adventure.

b) metaphor

Figurative Language
Similes, Metaphors
Quiz-Quiz-Trade

Instructions: Copy enough cards so each student has one card. Cut on dotted lines and fold in half.

Figurative Language—Similes, Metaphors

Question

The baby was like an octopus, grabbing at everything within reach.

This is an example of:
- a) simile
- b) metaphor

Figurative Language—Similes, Metaphors

Answer

The baby was like an octopus, grabbing at everything within reach.

a) simile

Figurative Language—Similes, Metaphors

Question

The sun is a yellow ball of fire.

This is an example of:
- a) simile
- b) metaphor

Figurative Language—Similes, Metaphors

Answer

The sun is a yellow ball of fire.

b) metaphor

Figurative Language—Similes, Metaphors

Question

The ship was like a small shell afloat on the sea.

This is an example of:
- a) simile
- b) metaphor

Figurative Language—Similes, Metaphors

Answer

The ship was like a small shell afloat on the sea.

a) simile

Figurative Language—Similes, Metaphors

Question

The fisherman had a face as wrinkled as an old boot.

This is an example of:
- a) simile
- b) metaphor

Figurative Language—Similes, Metaphors

Answer

The fisherman had a face as wrinkled as an old boot.

a) simile

Figurative Language
Similes, Metaphors
Quiz-Quiz-Trade

Instructions: Copy enough cards so each student has one card. Cut on dotted lines and fold in half.

Figurative Language—Similes, Metaphors

Question

The giant's steps were like thunder as he ran down the mountainside.

This is an example of:
  a) simile
  b) metaphor

Figurative Language—Similes, Metaphors

Answer

The giant's steps were like thunder as he ran down the mountainside.

a) simile

Figurative Language—Similes, Metaphors

Question

My feet are warm toast in my new wool socks.

This is an example of:
  a) simile
  b) metaphor

Figurative Language—Similes, Metaphors

Answer

My feet are warm toast in my new wool socks.

b) metaphor

Figurative Language—Similes, Metaphors

Question

The kitten was light as a feather.

This is an example of:
  a) simile
  b) metaphor

Figurative Language—Similes, Metaphors

Answer

The kitten was light as a feather.

a) simile

Figurative Language—Similes, Metaphors

Question

The white flowers were popcorn sprinkled on the grassy hillside.

This is an example of:
  a) simile
  b) metaphor

Figurative Language—Similes, Metaphors

Answer

The white flowers were popcorn sprinkled on the grassy hillside.

b) metaphor

Figurative Language
Similes, Metaphors
Quiz-Quiz-Trade

Instructions: Copy enough cards so each student has one card. Cut on dotted lines and fold in half.

Figurative Language—Similes, Metaphors	Figurative Language—Similes, Metaphors

Question
 	
She floated into the room like a cloud.
 	
This is an example of:
   a) simile
   b) metaphor
	Answer
	She floated into the room like a cloud.
	
	## a) simile

Question
 	
He was a limp dishrag.
 	
This is an example of:
   a) simile
   b) metaphor
	Answer
	He was a limp dishrag.
	
	## b) metaphor

Question
 	
My new pillow was like a huge cotton ball.
 	
This is an example of:
   a) simile
   b) metaphor
	Answer
	My new pillow was like a huge cotton ball.
	
	## a) simile

Question
 	
His feet were big boats.
 	
This is an example of:
   a) simile
   b) metaphor
	Answer
	His feet were big boats.
	
	## b) metaphor

Figurative Language
Similes, Metaphors
Quiz-Quiz-Trade

Instructions: Copy enough cards so each student has one card. Cut on dotted lines and fold in half.

Figurative Language—Similes, Metaphors

Question

The snow was as soft as sifted flour.

This is an example of:
    a) simile
    b) metaphor

Figurative Language—Similes, Metaphors

Answer

The snow was as soft as sifted flour.

a) simile

Figurative Language—Similes, Metaphors

Question

He seems gruff, but he's really just an old pussycat.

This is an example of:
    a) simile
    b) metaphor

Figurative Language—Similes, Metaphors

Answer

He seems gruff, but he's really just an old pussycat.

b) metaphor

Figurative Language—Similes, Metaphors

Question

That man is like a clever fox.

This is an example of:
    a) simile
    b) metaphor

Figurative Language—Similes, Metaphors

Answer

That man is like a clever fox.

a) simile

Figurative Language—Similes, Metaphors

Question

The soap was a slippery fish in the bathtub.

This is an example of:
    a) simile
    b) metaphor

Figurative Language—Similes, Metaphors

Answer

The soap was a slippery fish in the bathtub.

b) metaphor

Figurative Language
Similes, Metaphors
Quiz-Quiz-Trade

Instructions: Copy enough cards so each student has one card. Cut on dotted lines and fold in half.

Figurative Language—Similes, Metaphors

Question

The river was as clear as the sky.

This is an example of:
- a) simile
- b) metaphor

Figurative Language—Similes, Metaphors

Answer
The river was as clear as the sky.

a) simile

Figurative Language—Similes, Metaphors

Question

The hurricane scattered our lives like leaves in an autumn wind.

This is an example of:
- a) simile
- b) metaphor

Figurative Language—Similes, Metaphors

Answer
The hurricane scattered our lives like leaves in an autumn wind.

a) simile

Figurative Language—Similes, Metaphors

Question

The sky looks like a blue bowl filled with popcorn.

This is an example of:
- a) simile
- b) metaphor

Figurative Language—Similes, Metaphors

Answer
The sky looks like a blue bowl filled with popcorn.

a) simile

Figurative Language—Similes, Metaphors

Question

Sailboats were corks bobbing on the waves.

This is an example of:
- a) simile
- b) metaphor

Figurative Language—Similes, Metaphors

Answer
Sailboats were corks bobbing on the waves.

b) metaphor

Figurative Language
Alliteration, Idiom, Onomatopoeia, Hyperbole, Metaphor, Simile
Quiz-Quiz-Trade

Instructions: Copy enough cards so each student has one card. Cut on dotted lines and fold in half.

Figurative Language

Question

I told myself a <u>thousand</u> <u>times</u>, "Don't be scared!"

This is an example of:
    a) hyperbole
    b) onomatopoeia

Figurative Language

Answer

I told myself a <u>thousand</u> <u>times</u>, "Don't be scared!"

a) hyperbole

Figurative Language

Question

The giant's footsteps were thunder on the forest path.

This is an example of:
    a) alliteration
    b) metaphor

Figurative Language

Answer

The giant's footsteps were thunder on the forest path.

b) metaphor

Figurative Language

Question

Mrs. Smith's eyes flashed like lightning.

This is an example of:
    a) simile
    b) alliteration

Figurative Language

Answer

Mrs. Smith's eyes flashed like lightning.

a) simile

Figurative Language

Question

All eyes were glued to the TV.

This is an example of:
    a) idiom
    b) simile

Figurative Language

Answer

All eyes were glued to the TV.

a) idiom

Figurative Language

Alliteration, Idiom, Onomatopoeia, Hyperbole, Metaphor, Simile
Quiz-Quiz-Trade

Instructions: Copy enough cards so each student has one card. Cut on dotted lines and fold in half.

Figurative Language

Question

Green grass is growing and grasshoppers are everywhere this spring.

This is an example of:
a) alliteration
b) onomatopoeia

Figurative Language

Answer

Green grass is growing and grasshoppers are everywhere this spring.

a) alliteration

Figurative Language

Question

Peep! Peep! The chicks are hatching.

This is an example of:
a) idiom
b) onomatopoeia

Figurative Language

Answer

Peep! Peep! The chicks are hatching.

b) onomatopoeia

Figurative Language

Question

I counted a <u>million</u> sheep before I fell asleep last night.

This is an example of:
a) hyperbole
b) simile

Figurative Language

Answer

I counted a <u>million</u> sheep before I fell asleep last night.

a) hyperbole

Figurative Language

Question

My cat is such a feather, I could carry her around for hours.

This is an example of:
a) metaphor
b) alliteration

Figurative Language

Answer

My cat is such a feather, I could carry her around for hours.

a) metaphor

Figurative Language

Alliteration, Idiom, Onomatopoeia, Hyperbole, Metaphor, Simile

Quiz-Quiz-Trade

Instructions: Copy enough cards so each student has one card. Cut on dotted lines and fold in half.

Figurative Language

Question

The freezing rain stung like needles.

This is an example of:
    a) simile
    b) onomatopoeia

Figurative Language

Answer

The freezing rain stung like needles.

a) simile

Figurative Language

Question

Don't be so down in the dumps.

This is an example of:
    a) hyperbole
    b) idiom

Figurative Language

Answer

Don't be so down in the dumps.

b) idiom

Figurative Language

Question

Splash! The frog jumped into the pond.

This is an example of:
    a) onomatopoeia
    b) simile

Figurative Language

Answer

Splash! The frog jumped into the pond.

a) onomatopoeia

Figurative Language

Question

Mrs. White has x-ray vision—she knows what you are thinking.

This is an example of:
    a) hyperbole
    b) simile

Figurative Language

Answer

Mrs. White has x-ray vision—she knows what you are thinking.

a) hyperbole

Figurative Language

Alliteration, Idiom, Onomatopoeia, Hyperbole, Metaphor, Simile

Quiz-Quiz-Trade

Instructions: Copy enough cards so each student has one card. Cut on dotted lines and fold in half.

Figurative Language

Question

That assignment was a piece of cake.

This is an example of:
a) hyperbole
b) idiom

Figurative Language

Answer

That assignment was a piece of cake.

b) idiom

Figurative Language

Question

I laughed my head off at the movie.

This is an example of:
a) idiom
b) simile

Figurative Language

Answer

I laughed my head off at the movie.

a) idiom

Figurative Language

Question

The pillow was a cloud to my head.

This is an example of:
a) hyperbole
b) metaphor

Figurative Language

Answer

The pillow was a cloud to my head.

b) metaphor

Figurative Language

Question

Bzzzz—the bee hummed around my head.

This is an example of:
a) idiom
b) onomatopoeia

Figurative Language-Similes, Metaphors

Answer

Bzzzz—the bee hummed around my head.

b) onomatopoeia

Figurative Language
Alliteration, Idiom, Onomatopoeia, Hyperbole, Metaphor, Simile
Quiz-Quiz-Trade

Instructions: Copy enough cards so each student has one card. Cut on dotted lines and fold in half.

Figurative Language

Question

Ted was a nervous cat as he worried about his appointment.

This is an example of:
    a) simile
    b) metaphor

Figurative Language

Answer

Ted was a nervous cat as he worried about his appointment.

b) metaphor

Figurative Language

Question

"Lighten up!" my mother told me.

This is an example of:
    a) hyperbole
    b) idiom

Figurative Language

Answer

"Lighten up!" my mother told me.

b) idiom

Figurative Language

Question

My teacher showered me with praises.

This is an example of:
    a) idiom
    b) alliteration

Figurative Language

Answer

My teacher showered me with praises.

a) idiom

Figurative Language

Question

Whirling winds and wild waves washed many seashells to the shore.

This is an example of:
    a) alliteration
    b) idiom

Figurative Language

Answer

Whirling winds and wild waves washed many seashells to the shore.

a) alliteration

Balanced Literacy • Third Grade • Skidmore & Graber
Kagan Publishing • 1 (800) 933-2667 • www.KaganOnline.com

Figurative Language

Alliteration, Idiom, Onomatopoeia, Hyperbole, Metaphor, Simile

Quiz-Quiz-Trade

Instructions: Copy enough cards so each student has one card. Cut on dotted lines and fold in half.

Figurative Language	Figurative Language
Question "Shhh! We must have it quiet in the library." This is an example of: a) alliteration b) onomatopoeia	**Answer** "Shhh! We must have it quiet in the library." **b) onomatopoeia**
Question The flowers in the garden were a rainbow of color. This is an example of: a) idiom b) metaphor	**Answer** The bar of soap was a slippery eel in the bathtub. **b) metaphor**
Question My answer was a shot in the dark. This is an example of: a) onomatopoeia b) idiom	**Answer** My answer was a shot in the dark. **b) idiom**
Question He's as dry as a desert. This is an example of: a) simile b) idiom	**Answer** He's as dry as a desert. **a) simile**

Figurative Language

Alliteration, Idiom, Onomatopoeia, Hyperbole, Metaphor, Simile
Quiz-Quiz-Trade

Instructions: Copy enough cards so each student has one card. Cut on dotted lines and fold in half.

Figurative Language

Question

"Whoo-whoo-whoo!" The owl kept me awake most of the night.

This is an example of:
    a) onomatopoeia
    b) metaphor

Figurative Language

Answer

"Whoo-whoo-whoo!" The owl kept me awake most of the night.

a) onomatopoeia

Figurative Language

Question

She was as funny as a clown when she told the joke.

This is an example of:
    a) simile
    b) onomatopoeia

Figurative Language

Answer

She was as funny as a clown when she told the joke.

a) simile

Figurative Language

Question

My grandfather really knows how to stretch a dollar.

This is an example of:
    a) simile
    b) idiom

Figurative Language

Answer

My grandfather really knows how to stretch a dollar.

b) idiom

Figurative Language

Question

I had so much homework, I needed a trailer to get my books home.

This is an example of:
    a) hyperbole
    b) alliteration

Figurative Language

Answer

I had so much homework, I needed a trailer to get my books home.

a) hyperbole

Figurative Language

Alliteration, Idiom, Onomatopoeia, Hyperbole, Metaphor, Simile

Quiz-Quiz-Trade

Instructions: Copy enough cards so each student has one card. Cut on dotted lines and fold in half.

Figurative Language

Question

Two minutes before the audition, Anna got cold feet.

This is an example of:
    a) simile
    b) idiom

Figurative Language

Answer

Two minutes before the audition, Anna got cold feet.

b) idiom

Figurative Language

Question

"Vrooom, vroom, the race car sped by on the quiet street."

This is an example of:
    a) onomatopoeia
    b) hyperbole

Figurative Language

Answer

"Vrooom, vroom, the race car sped by on the quiet street."

a) onomatopoeia

Figurative Language

Question

It was so cold, even the polar bears were wearing jackets.

This is an example of:
    a) hyperbole
    b) simile

Figurative Language

Answer

It was so cold, even the polar bears were wearing jackets.

a) hyperbole

Figurative Language

Question

I could have died, I was so embarrassed.

This is an example of:
    a) simile
    b) hyperbole

Figurative Language

Answer

I could have died, I was so embarrassed.

b) hyperbole

Figurative Language
Alliteration, Idiom, Onomatopoeia, Hyperbole, Metaphor, Simile
Quiz-Quiz-Trade

Instructions: Copy enough cards so each student has one card. Cut on dotted lines and fold in half.

Figurative Language
 	
Question
 	
Tim had to eat crow when he found out the truth.
 	
This is an example of:
    a) idiom
    b) simile
	Figurative Language
	
	Answer
	Tim had to eat crow when he found out the truth.
	
	## a) idiom

Figurative Language
 	
Question
 	
Kate's as proud as a peacock about her reward.
 	
This is an example of:
    a) simile
    b) onomatopoeia
	Figurative Language
	
	Answer
	Kate's as proud as a peacock about her reward.
	
	## a) simile

Figurative Language
 	
Question
 	
Silvery shadows slid silently.
 	
This is an example of:
    a) alliteration
    b) simile
	Figurative Language
	
	Answer
	Silvery shadows slid silently.
	
	## a) alliteration

Figurative Language
 	
Question
 	
The basketball team got taken to the cleaners when they played their rivals.
 	
This is an example of:
    a) onomatopoeia
    b) idiom
	Figurative Language
	
	Answer
	The basketball team got taken to the cleaners when they played their rivals.
	
	## b) idiom

Figurative Language

Alliteration, Idiom, Onomatopoeia, Hyperbole, Metaphor, Simile

Quiz-Quiz-Trade

Instructions: Copy enough cards so each student has one card. Cut on dotted lines and fold in half.

Figurative Language

Question

Sam saw sailboats sailing slowly along the shore.

This is an example of:
    a) onomatopoeia
    b) alliteration

Figurative Language

Answer

Sam saw sailboats sailing slowly along the shore.

b) alliteration

Figurative Language

Question

"Grrrr, grrrr!" A low growl came from the beastly watchdog as I walked by the fence.

This is an example of:
    a) hyperbole
    b) onomatopoeia

Figurative Language

Answer

"Grrrr, grrrr!" A low growl came from the beastly watchdog as I walked by the fence.

b) onomatopoeia

Figurative Language

Question

The trees stood tall as statues against the night sky.

This is an example of:
    a) simile
    b) idiom

Figurative Language

Answer

The trees stood tall as statues against the night sky.

a) simile

Figurative Language

Question

The test was so hard, by the time I finished I was a hundred years old.

This is an example of:
    a) alliteration
    b) hyperbole

Figurative Language

Answer

The test was so hard, by the time I finished I was a hundred years old.

b) hyperbole

Homophone Definitions
Quiz-Quiz-Trade

Instructions: Copy enough cards so each student has one card. Cut on dotted lines and fold in half.

Homophone Definitions

Question

cent

a) a coin worth one penny
b) asked to go

Homophone Definitions

Answer

cent

a) a coin worth one penny

Homophone Definitions

Question

sent

a) a coin worth one penny
b) asked to go

Homophone Definitions

Answer

sent

b) asked to go

Homophone Definitions

Question

ring

a) to twist and squeeze
b) a circular object

Homophone Definitions

Answer

ring

b) a circular object

Homophone Definitions

Question

wring

a) to twist and squeeze
b) a circular object

Homophone Definitions

Answer

wring

a) to twist and squeeze

Homophone Definitions
Quiz-Quiz-Trade

Instructions: Copy enough cards so each student has one card. Cut on dotted lines and fold in half.

Homophone Definitions	Homophone Definitions
Question	**Answer**
groan	**groan**
a) to make a moaning sound b) to increase in size	a) to make a moaning sound

Homophone Definitions	Homophone Definitions
Question	**Answer**
grown	**grown**
a) to make a moaning sound b) to increase in size	b) to increase in size

Homophone Definitions	Homophone Definitions
Question	**Answer**
days	**days**
a) to stun or dazzle b) a period of time	b) a period of time

Homophone Definitions	Homophone Definitions
Question	**Answer**
daze	**daze**
a) to stun or dazzle b) a period of time	a) to stun or dazzle

Homophone Definitions
Quiz-Quiz-Trade

Instructions: Copy enough cards so each student has one card. Cut on dotted lines and fold in half.

Homophone Definitions	Homophone Definitions
Question **berry** a) a small fruit b) to place in the ground	**Answer** **berry** a) a small fruit
Question **bury** a) a small fruit b) to place in the ground	**Answer** **bury** b) to place in the ground
Question **break** a) to slow down b) to crack into pieces	**Answer** **break** b) to crack into pieces
Question **brake** a) to slow down b) to crack into pieces	**Answer** **brake** a) to slow down

104 Balanced Literacy • Third Grade • Skidmore & Graber
 Kagan Publishing • 1 (800) 933-2667 • www.KaganOnline.com

Homophone Definitions
Quiz-Quiz-Trade

Instructions: Copy enough cards so each student has one card. Cut on dotted lines and fold in half.

Homophone Definitions	Homophone Definitions
Question	**Answer**
clothes	**clothes**
a) to shut b) things to wear	b) things to wear

Homophone Definitions	Homophone Definitions
Question	**Answer**
close	**close**
a) to shut b) things to wear	a) to shut

Homophone Definitions	Homophone Definitions
Question	**Answer**
rain	**rain**
a) moisture falling from the sky b) to rule	a) moisture falling from the sky

Homophone Definitions	Homophone Definitions
Question	**Answer**
reign	**reign**
a) moisture falling from the sky b) to rule	b) to rule

Homophone Definitions
Quiz-Quiz-Trade

Instructions: Copy enough cards so each student has one card. Cut on dotted lines and fold in half.

Homophone Definitions	Homophone Definitions
Question **roll** a) the part played by an actor b) to turn over and over	**Answer** **roll** b) to turn over and over
Question **role** a) the part played by an actor b) to turn over and over	**Answer** **role** a) the part played by an actor
Question **way** a) to measure heaviness b) road or path	**Answer** **way** b) road or path
Question **weigh** a) to measure heaviness b) road or path	**Answer** **weigh** a) to measure heaviness

Homophone Definitions
Quiz-Quiz-Trade

Instructions: Copy enough cards so each student has one card. Cut on dotted lines and fold in half.

Homophone Definitions	Homophone Definitions
Question **sale** a) lowered prices b) to move across the water	**Answer** **sale** a) lowered prices
Question **sail** a) lowered prices b) to move across the water	**Answer** **sail** b) to move across the water
Question **steel** a) a strong metal b) to take something	**Answer** **steel** a) a strong metal
Question **steal** a) a strong metal b) to take something	**Answer** **steal** b) to take something

Homophone Definitions
Quiz-Quiz-Trade

Instructions: Copy enough cards so each student has one card. Cut on dotted lines and fold in half.

Homophone Definitions	Homophone Definitions
Question	**Answer**
Knows	**Knows**
a) body part used to smell b) to be familiar with	b) to be familiar with

Homophone Definitions	Homophone Definitions
Question	**Answer**
nose	**nose**
a) body part used to smell b) to be familiar with	a) body part used to smell

Homophone Definitions	Homophone Definitions
Question	**Answer**
hoarse	**hoarse**
a) a low croaking sound b) a large mammal used to ride	a) a low croaking sound

Homophone Definitions	Homophone Definitions
Question	**Answer**
horse	**horse**
a) a low croaking sound b) a large mammal used to ride	b) a large mammal used to ride

Homophone Sentences

Quiz-Quiz-Trade

Instructions: Copy enough cards so each student has one card. Cut on dotted lines and fold in half.

Homophone Sentences	Homophone Sentences
Question	**Answer**
Jake paid one _____ for the candy.	Jake paid one <u>cent</u> for the candy.
a) cent b) sent	a) cent

Homophone Sentences	Homophone Sentences
Question	**Answer**
We _____ a package in the mail.	We <u>sent</u> a package in the mail.
a) cent b) sent	b) sent

Homophone Sentences	Homophone Sentences
Question	**Answer**
Mary wore a _____ on her finger.	Mary wore a <u>ring</u> on her finger.
a) wring b) ring	b) ring

Homophone Sentences	Homophone Sentences
Question	**Answer**
John will _____ the washcloth.	John will <u>wring</u> the washcloth.
a) wring b) ring	a) wring

Homophone Sentences
Quiz-Quiz-Trade

Instructions: Copy enough cards so each student has one card. Cut on dotted lines and fold in half.

Homophone Sentences	**Homophone Sentences**
Question A _____ was heard from the crowd. a) groan b) grown	Answer A <u>groan</u> was heard from the crowd. a) groan
Homophone Sentences	**Homophone Sentences**
Question You have _____ at least an inch. a) groan b) grown	Answer You have <u>grown</u> at least an inch. b) grown
Homophone Sentences	**Homophone Sentences**
Question There are seven _____ in a week. a) daze b) days	Answer There are seven <u>days</u> in a week. b) days
Homophone Sentences	**Homophone Sentences**
Question Phil was in a _____ after his nap. a) daze b) days	Answer Phil was in a <u>daze</u> after his nap. a) daze

Homophone Sentences
Quiz-Quiz-Trade

Instructions: Copy enough cards so each student has one card. Cut on dotted lines and fold in half.

Homophone Sentences

Question

The girl picked a red _____ from the bush.

a) bury
b) berry

Homophone Sentences

Answer

The girl picked a red <u>berry</u> from the bush.

b) berry

Homophone Sentences

Question

Rex, the dog, will _____ his bone.

a) bury
b) berry

Homophone Sentences

Answer

Rex, the dog, will <u>bury</u> his bone.

a) bury

Homophone Sentences

Question

The dish will _____ if you drop it.

a) brake
b) break

Homophone Sentences

Answer

The dish will <u>break</u> if you drop it.

b) break

Homophone Sentences

Question

Use the _____ to stop the car.

a) brake
b) break

Homophone Sentences

Answer

Use the <u>brake</u> to stop the car.

a) brake

Homophone Sentences
Quiz-Quiz-Trade

Instructions: Copy enough cards so each student has one card. Cut on dotted lines and fold in half.

Homophone Sentences	Homophone Sentences
Question Please _____ the door to the house. a) close b) clothes	**Answer** Please <u>close</u> the door to the house. a) close
Question Which _____ will you wear? a) close b) clothes	**Answer** Which <u>clothes</u> will you wear? b) clothes
Question The _____ caused a flood. a) rain b) reign	**Answer** The <u>rain</u> caused a flood. a) rain
Question The King will _____ over the country. a) rain b) reign	**Answer** The King will <u>reign</u> over the country. b) reign

Balanced Literacy • Third Grade • Skidmore & Graber
Kagan Publishing • 1 (800) 933-2667 • www.KaganOnline.com

Homophone Sentences
Quiz-Quiz-Trade

Instructions: Copy enough cards so each student has one card. Cut on dotted lines and fold in half.

Homophone Sentences	Homophone Sentences
Question The ball will _____ down the steep hill. a) roll b) role	**Answer** The ball will <u>roll</u> down the steep hill. a) roll
Question What _____ will you play in the movie? a) roll b) role	**Answer** What <u>role</u> will you play in the movie? b) role
Question We will use a map to find the _____. a) weigh b) way	**Answer** We will use a map to find the <u>way</u>. b) way
Question The scale will tell you how much you _____. a) weigh b) way	**Answer** The scale will tell you how much you <u>weigh</u>. a) weigh

Homophone Sentences
Quiz-Quiz-Trade

Instructions: Copy enough cards so each student has one card. Cut on dotted lines and fold in half.

Homophone Sentences	Homophone Sentences
Question The boat will _____ around the lake. a) sale b) sail	**Answer** The boat will <u>sail</u> around the lake. b) sail
Question We bought the shoes during a _____. a) sale b) sail	**Answer** We bought the shoes during a <u>sale</u>. a) sale
Question The skyscraper was made of _____. a) steal b) steel	**Answer** The skyscraper was made of <u>steel</u>. b) steel
Question The squirrel will _____ the birdseed. a) steal b) steel	**Answer** The squirrel will <u>steal</u> the birdseed. a) steal

Homophone Sentences
Quiz-Quiz-Trade

Instructions: Copy enough cards so each student has one card. Cut on dotted lines and fold in half.

Homophone Sentences

Question

Sue already _____ the song.

a) knows
b) nose

Homophone Sentences

Answer

Sue already <u>knows</u> the song.

a) knows

Homophone Sentences

Question

Sid smelled the cookies with his _____.

a) knows
b) nose

Homophone Sentences

Answer

Sid smelled the cookies with his <u>nose</u>.

b) nose

Homophone Sentences

Question

Mandy had a _____ voice from yelling.

a) horse
b) hoarse

Homophone Sentences

Answer

Mandy had a <u>hoarse</u> voice from yelling.

b) hoarse

Homophone Sentences

Question

Let's ride the _____ in the parade.

a) horse
b) hoarse

Homophone Sentences

Answer

Let's ride the <u>horse</u> in the parade.

a) horse

Homophone Sentences
Quiz-Quiz-Trade

Instructions: Copy enough cards so each student has one card. Cut on dotted lines and fold in half.

Homophone Sentences

Question

This is _____ a good time to talk loudly.

a) knot
b) not

Homophone Sentences

Answer

This is <u>not</u> a good time to talk loudly.

b) not

Homophone Sentences

Question

Help me untie the _____ in my shoelace.

a) knot
b) not

Homophone Sentences

Answer

Help me untie the <u>knot</u> in my shoelace.

a) knot

Homophone Sentences

Question

Tell me a _____ about the princess.

a) tale
b) tail

Homophone Sentences

Answer

Tell me a <u>tale</u> about the princess.

a) tale

Homophone Sentences

Question

The puppy wagged his _____.

a) tale
b) tail

Homophone Sentences

Answer

The puppy wagged his <u>tail</u>.

b) tail

Balanced Literacy • Third Grade • Skidmore & Graber
Kagan Publishing • 1 (800) 933-2667 • www.KaganOnline.com

Pick A Card, Any Card

Using a Fan-N-Pick Mat and question cards, students play Fan-N-Pick to identify text features, answer story elements questions, and preview nonfiction.

STRUCTURE
Fan-N-Pick

Activity Steps

1. Each team receives the Fan-N-Pick Mat, an identical text for each student on the team, and a set of cards.

2. The Fan-N-Pick Mat is placed in the center of the team table, with each corner pointing to a student.

3. Student #1 (Fan) holds question cards in a fan and says, "Pick a card, any card!"

4. Student #2 (Pick and Read) picks a card, reads the question aloud, and allows think time.

5. Student #3 (Answer) responds orally and/or shows the answer.

6. Student #4 (Check and Praise) responds to the answer by tutoring or praising.

7. The Fan-N-Pick Mat is rotated one person clockwise for each new round, indicating each student's new role.

Blacklines

Fan-N-Pick Mat

Instructions: Cut out this mat and place it in the center of the team. Each corner points to a student, indicating his/her role for that round of Fan-N-Pick. For each new round, rotate the mat clockwise one position, indicating each student's new role for that round.

Fan

Pick and Read

Fan-N-Pick Mat

Check and Praise

Answer

Text Features
Fan-N-Pick

Instructions: Copy one set of cards for each team. Cut apart. Use with Fan-N-Pick Mat.

Text Features	Text Features	Text Features
Find or locate a: Bullet	**Find or locate a:** Bold Word	**Find or locate a:** Map
Find or locate a: Timeline	**Find or locate a:** Boxed Item	**Find or locate a:** Chart

Text Features
Fan-N-Pick

Instructions: Copy one set of cards for each team. Cut apart. Use with Fan-N-Pick Mat.

Text Features	Text Features	Text Features
Find or locate a: Graph	**Find or locate a:** Diagram	**Find or locate an:** Index
Find or locate a: Caption	**Find or locate an:** Italicized Word	**Find or locate a:** Sidebar

Text Features
Fan-N-Pick

Instructions: Copy one set of cards for each team. Cut apart. Use with Fan-N-Pick Mat.

Text Features	Text Features	Text Features
Find or locate a:	**Find or locate a:**	**Find or locate a:**
Photograph	Colored Word	Stylized Word

Text Features	Text Features	Text Features
Find or locate a:	**Find or locate a:**	**Find or locate a:**
Table of Contents	Heading	Glossary

Story Elements (Fiction)

Fan-N-Pick

Instructions: Copy one set of cards for each team. Cut apart. Use with Fan-N-Pick Mat.

Story Elements (Fiction)	Story Elements (Fiction)	Story Elements (Fiction)
What is the title?	**Who is the author?**	**Who is the illustrator?**

Story Elements (Fiction)	Story Elements (Fiction)	Story Elements (Fiction)
What is the setting? · **Where?** · **When?**	**Who are the main characters?**	**What is the problem?**

Story Elements (Fiction)
Fan-N-Pick

Instructions: Copy one set of cards for each team. Cut apart. Use with Fan-N-Pick Mat.

Story Elements (Fiction)	Story Elements (Fiction)	Story Elements (Fiction)
What is the solution?	What happened in the beginning?	What happened in the middle?

Story Elements (Fiction)	Story Elements (Fiction)	Story Elements (Fiction)
What happened at the end?	What did you learn from the story?	Tell about one of the characters.

Previewing Before Reading (Nonfiction)
Fan-N-Pick

Instructions: Copy one set of cards for each team. Cut apart. Use with Fan-N-Pick Mat.

Previewing Before Reading (Nonfiction) Show a text feature in your text and name it.	**Previewing Before Reading (Nonfiction)** Show the text feature that you think will be most helpful to you when you read, and tell why.	**Previewing Before Reading (Nonfiction)** Choose one type of text feature used, and count the number of times it is used.
Previewing Before Reading (Nonfiction) Which table of contents item looks the most interesting? Why?	**Previewing Before Reading (Nonfiction)** Find a word that is new to you. Tell some strategies that you could use to help learn about the word.	**Previewing Before Reading (Nonfiction)** Why do you think the author wrote this text?

Previewing Before Reading (Nonfiction)

Fan-N-Pick

Instructions: Copy one set of cards for each team. Cut apart. Use with Fan-N-Pick Mat.

Previewing Before Reading (Nonfiction) **What would you like to learn from this text?**	**Previewing Before Reading (Nonfiction)** **What do you think this text is mainly about?**	**Previewing Before Reading (Nonfiction)** **How many <u>different</u> text features did the author use?**
Previewing Before Reading (Nonfiction) **Tell what you already know about the topic of the text.**	**Previewing Before Reading (Nonfiction)** **Ask a question you would like the text to answer. Start your question with Why...?**	**Previewing Before Reading (Nonfiction)** **Which text feature will you spend the most time studying? Why?**

Activity

Comprehension Cubes

Teammates roll a comprehension cube to ask and answer questions relating to a selected text. Students may respond in any order, but they must place their Talking Chip in the center of the team table to indicate they've participated.

Activity Steps

1. Each team receives one cube and a text selection. Each teammate receives one Talking Chip (any chip or token will work).

2. Student #1 rolls the comprehension cube and reads the question or formulates a question.

3. All students take turns responding to the question, placing their chip in the center when talking.

4. When all chips are used, teammates each collect their chips.

5. Student #2 rolls the cube and repeats from Step 2.

STRUCTURE

Talking Chips

Blacklines

Comprehension Question Cube
(Before Reading)

Instructions: Copy the cube pattern on cardstock. Cut out, fold, and tape together to form a cube.

What do you think the author wants us to learn from this text?

What do you already know about the topic of this text?

What type of text do you think this will be (fiction or nonfiction)? Why?

What does the cover or first page tell you?

What is one text feature that you think will be helpful? Why?

What would you expect to find out from reading this text?

Comprehension Question Cube
(After Reading)

Instructions: Copy the cube pattern on cardstock. Cut out, fold, and tape together to form a cube.

What would you like to know more about?

What did you learn that you did not know before?

Why do you think the author wrote this text?

Why do you think the information in this text is important?

What is one question you would like to ask the author?

What connection can you make to this text?

• Text to self
• Text to text
• Text to world

Comprehension Question Cube

(Reflection)

Instructions: Copy the cube pattern on cardstock. Cut out, fold, and tape together to form a cube.

What part of the text would you have changed? How and why?

What was your favorite part? Why?

What are you reminded of by the text?

What is something in the text, that you don't think could really happen? Why?

What was something in the text, that could really happen? Why?

What was a tricky word? How did you figure it out?

Questioning Cube

Instructions: Copy the cube pattern on cardstock. Cut out, fold, and tape together to form a cube.

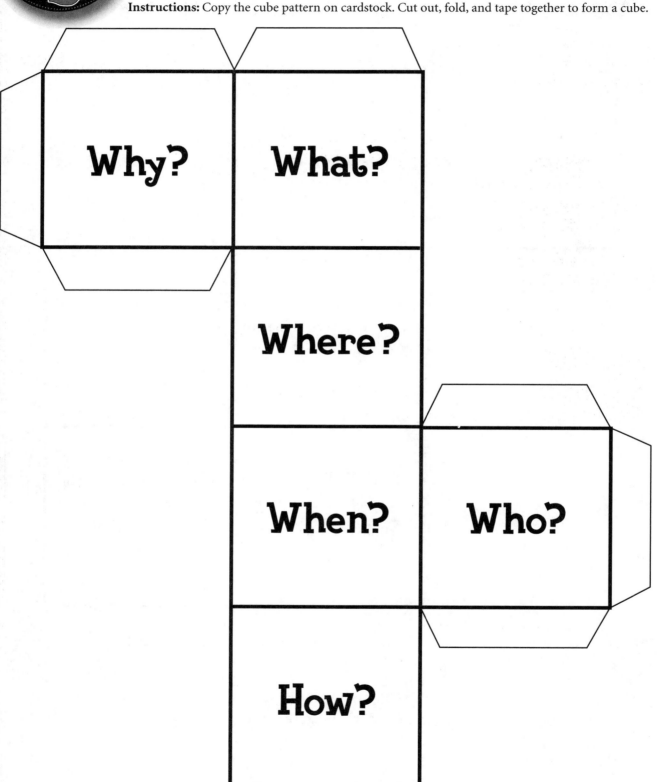

Spinning Vocabulary

Teammates use vocabulary cards and a spinner to learn vocabulary. This is a great way to examine vocabulary words from guided reading texts, teacher read-aloud texts and, content areas (social studies, science, math).

STRUCTURE

RoundTable Consensus

Activity Steps

1. Each team receives a set of Sentence Cards and a Vocabulary Spinner (next page) on cardstock with a plastic or metal spinner arrow (if not available, use a pencil and a paperclip). Every student needs a dictionary.

2. Student #1 picks a sentence card from the pile and reads it.

3. All students look up the underlined vocabulary word in the dictionary and read the definitions silently.

4. Student #2 selects the appropriate definition for the context, reads it, and states the reason for the choice.

5. Student #2 checks for consensus.

6. Teammates show agreement or lack of agreement with thumbs up or down.

7. If there is agreement, the students celebrate and Student #2 spins the spinner. Student #3 responds to the spinner's prompt and checks for consensus.

8. The process continues until time's up or the team has completed their vocabulary words.

Blacklines

Vocabulary Spinner
RoundTable Consensus

Instructions: Copy a spinner on cardstock for each team. Add a plastic/metal spinner in the middle or use a spinner made from a paper clip and a pencil. (To make a paper clip spinner: Place a paper clip over the center of the spinner. Place the pencil point on the center point of the spinner, through the paper clip. Using the other hand, spin the paper clip around the pencil point.) Students take turns spinning the spinner and following the directions.

What is another word that means about the same as your word? (synonym)

Paraphrase the sentence.

Discuss the word:
· Visual clues
· Letter patterns
· Tricky parts

Use the word in a new sentence.

Sentence Cards for Vocabulary Spinner

RoundTable Consensus

Instructions: Copy one set of cards per team. Cut apart.

Sentence Cards for Vocabulary Spinner Once you blow out the candles on your birthday cake and they are <u>extinguished</u>, the wicks will still smoke for a few minutes.	**Sentence Cards for Vocabulary Spinner** The dentist had to <u>extract</u> the dying tooth that had been causing my grandmother much pain.	**Sentence Cards for Vocabulary Spinner** The longest hurricane on <u>record</u> happened in 1994 and lasted 31 days.
Sentence Cards for Vocabulary Spinner At noon today, the president will <u>declare</u> the person he has chosen for the position.	**Sentence Cards for Vocabulary Spinner** The <u>minimal</u> amount of time John spent practicing piano was evident when recital time came.	**Sentence Cards for Vocabulary Spinner** Mary spent extra time at recess to finish the paper her teacher marked, "<u>incomplete</u>."

Blank Sentence Cards
for Vocabulary Spinner

RoundTable Consensus

Instructions: Use blank cards to create sentence cards.

Blank Sentence Cards for Vocabulary Spinner	Blank Sentence Cards for Vocabulary Spinner	Blank Sentence Cards for Vocabulary Spinner

Blank Sentence Cards for Vocabulary Spinner	Blank Sentence Cards for Vocabulary Spinner	Blank Sentence Cards for Vocabulary Spinner

Activity

Comprehension Puzzles

After teammates have read the same text, teammates place puzzle pieces on a puzzle mat. Each puzzle piece has a prompt for students to review the reading. Three different puzzles blacklines are provided: 1) retelling fiction, 2) retelling nonfiction, and 3) nonfiction text features.

STRUCTURE

RoundTable Consensus

Activity Steps

1. Each team receives a set of puzzle pieces and a puzzle mat. The puzzle pieces are mixed up and placed facedown in the center of team.

2. Student #1 selects one puzzle piece, reads the prompt, and gives an answer. For example, if the puzzle piece is "Titles" the student states the title. The student checks for consensus.

3. Teammates show agreement or lack of agreement with thumbs up or down.

4. If there is agreement, the student places the puzzle piece on the matching section on the puzzle mat. If not, teammates discuss the response until there is agreement. If no agreement is reached, the puzzle piece is set aside to be discussed later.

5. The next student selects the next puzzle piece and the process is continued until the team completes the puzzle.

Blacklines

Retelling (Fiction) Puzzle Pieces

RoundTable Consensus

Instructions: Cut puzzle pieces apart.

2. Characters

Retelling (Fiction)

4. Problem

Retelling (Fiction)

8. Solution

Retelling (Fiction)

3. Setting

Retelling (Fiction)

7. Event

Retelling (Fiction)

1. Title

5. Event

Retelling (Fiction)

6. Event

Retelling (Fiction)

Retelling (Fiction) Puzzle Mat
RoundTable Consensus

Instructions: Copy one puzzle mat for each team.

4

8

2

3

7

1

5

6

Retelling (Nonfiction) Puzzle Pieces
RoundTable Consensus

Instructions: Cut puzzle pieces apart.

Detail

Retelling (Nonfiction)

Text Feature

Retelling (Nonfiction)

Detail

Retelling (Nonfiction)

Detail

Retelling (Nonfiction)

Information from Picture

Retelling (Nonfiction)

Heading (Main Idea)

Retelling (Nonfiction)

Text Feature

Retelling (Nonfiction)

Key Vocabulary Words

Retelling (Nonfiction)

Retelling (Nonfiction) Puzzle Mat
RoundTable Consensus

Instructions: Copy one puzzle mat for each team.

Text Feature (Nonfiction) Puzzle Pieces
RoundTable Consensus

Instructions: Cut puzzle pieces apart.

(Bolded, Italicized, Colored, or Stylized) Word
Text Feature (Nonfiction)

Table of Contents
Text Feature (Nonfiction)

Timeline
Text Feature (Nonfiction)

Heading
Text Feature (Nonfiction)

Index
Text Feature (Nonfiction)

Map
Text Feature (Nonfiction)

Photograph with Caption
Text Feature (Nonfiction)

Glossary
Text Feature (Nonfiction)

Label
Text Feature (Nonfiction)

Bullets
Text Feature (Nonfiction)

Boxed Item or Sidebar
Text Feature (Nonfiction)

Graph or Diagram
Text Feature (Nonfiction)

Balanced Literacy • Third Grade • Skidmore & Graber
Kagan Publishing • 1 (800) 933-2667 • www.KaganOnline.com

Text Feature (Nonfiction) Puzzle Mat
RoundTable Consensus

Instructions: Copy one puzzle mat for each team.

Activity

Anticipation Guide

Before reading a text, partners take turns marking "true" or "false" predictions on an Anticipation Guide Form. Students read the text independently and mark their answers and page number where the answer was found on the "after reading" section. Partners then take turns sharing their answers and proving it from the text. Students are allowed to adjust answers after discussion with partner.

Activity Steps

1 Using an Anticipation Guide Student Form, the teacher fills in statements relating to the reading, some true and some false. (See the Anticipation Guide Sample on page 143.)

2 Pairs receive an Anticipation Guide Form and a book or article to read.

3 Before reading the text, partners take turns making true or false predictions for each statement on the form by checking the "true" or "false" box in the "Before Reading" column.

4 Students read the assigned article or book independently.

5 After reading the text, Partner A reads the first statement on the Anticipation Guide, then finds the related text page. Partner A states if the statement is true or false and, when Partner B agrees, records the page and checks the "true" or "false" box in the "After Reading" column.

6 Partners alternate roles for each statement.

STRUCTURE
RallyTable & RallyCoach

Blacklines

Anticipation Guide Sample

RallyTable Before Reading		Ranger Rick March 2004 pg. 22–28 "Roach! The Insect We Love to Hate"	RallyCoach After Reading		
True	False		Pg.	True	False
	✓	1. Cockroaches have been around for 350 million years.	23	✓	
✓		2. Cockroaches will eat paper, leather, and even wood.	23	✓	
✓		3. Many children and adults are allergic to bits of old, dried up cockroach skin.	25	✓	
✓		4. All cockroach mothers carry their eggs inside their bodies and the young are born live.	25		✓
✓		5. The American cockroach can go without water for three months as long as it has food.	26		✓
	✓	6. Cockroaches are very picky about the food they eat.	26		✓
✓		7. Some reptiles, like mice, opossums, and bats, eat cockroaches.	27		✓
	✓	8. There are over 4,000 different kinds of cockroaches.	28	✓	
	✓	9. All cockroaches are smaller than a penny.	28		✓
	✓	10. Cockroaches are either brown or black.	28		✓
	✓	11. Some cockroaches use suction cups between their claws to walk up glass.	23	✓	
✓		12. Americans spend millions of dollars every year to try to get rid of cockroaches.	22	✓	
✓		13. Cockroaches have fast reactions and very good senses such as smell, taste, and sound.	23	✓	

Do you have a question to ask the group?

Anticipation Guide Student Form

RallyTable Before Reading		Name of Article_____ Magazine Title_____ Date_____ Pg. _____	RallyCoach After Reading		
True	False		Pg.	True	False
		1.			
		2.			
		3.			
		4.			
		5.			
		6.			
		7.			
		8.			
		9.			
		10.			
		11.			
		12.			
		13.			

Do you have a question to ask the group?

Sketching for Comprehension

Students listen to the teacher, sketch the important details, share their sketches, then draft a main idea of the statement.

STRUCTURE

Listen-Sketch-Draft

Activity Steps

1. Each student is given the Listen-Sketch-Draft form.

2. The teacher presents the first chunk of information while students listen carefully.

3. The teacher stops presenting and calls for each student to sketch the most important details in the first "sketch" box.

4. Students share their sketches using RoundRobin or Timed Pair Share.

5. Students draft a main idea statement in the first "draft" box.

6. The process is repeated for additional chunks of information.

7. When all chunks of information have been presented, students draft a summary in the bottom box.

8. Students compare their summaries with a partner or teammate.

Blacklines

Listen-Sketch-Draft
Sample

Important to Remember (Sketch)	Main Idea (Draft)
	Sea otters are mammals.
	Sea otters live in kelp forests.
	They eat: • sea urchins • fish • clams • abalone

Summary Statement:
Sea otters are mammals that live in kelp forests in the sea. They eat sea urchins, fish, clams, and abalone. Sea otters help the kelp forests by eating these creatures.

Listen-Sketch-Draft
Form

Instructions: Copy for each student.

Important to Remember (Sketch)	Main Idea (Draft)

Summary Statement:

Story Predictions

Students manipulate cards with possible characters, settings, problems, and solutions to the text on the prediction mat. They confirm or adjust their predictions during reading and after reading the selection. Partners take timed turns listening and sharing about their Prediction Mats.

Activity Steps

1) The teacher creates Story Element Cards corresponding to the story the class will read. (Two sample sets are provided.)

2) Each student receives a Prediction Mat and a set of story cards.

3) As the story is read, students are stopped periodically and given time to make story predictions by manipulating their Story Cards on their Prediction Mats. Stories can be read using:
   • Teacher read aloud
   • RallyRobin reading (partners take turns)
   • Independent reading

4) After each prediction adjustment, students are each given one minute to share their prediction with a partner.

STRUCTURE

Timed Pair Share

Blacklines

Prediction Mat

Timed Pair Share

Instructions: Copy for each student.

Characters	Setting

Problem	Solution

Important Words

Blank Story Element Cards for Prediction Mat
Timed Pair Share

Instructions: Teacher writes possible story elements in these boxes and makes copies for each student.

Story Element Cards for Prediction Mat
Timed Pair Share
Because of Winn-Dixie by Kate DiCamillo

Instructions: Copy for each student. Cut apart.

Opal	Winn-Dixie	friendship	Preacher
Witch	music	Florida	Litmus Lozenge
Thunderstorm	Mrs. Franny Block	Dewberry boys	Gertrude's Pets
party	sorrow	pickles	guitar
Gloria Dump	Otis	Amanda	ten things
Sweetie Pie	library	garden	bottles

Story Element Cards for Prediction Mat
Timed Pair Share
Fly Away Home by Eve Bunting

Instructions: Copy for each student. Cut apart.

escalator	janitor	bird	airplanes
security guards	baggage	dad	boy
terminal	notebook	Idaho Joe	free
dead time	Mrs. Medina	homeless	shoe
noticed	airport	home	mom
sad	rent	money	open door

Sort It Out

Teammates cover a mat with ideas about what they just read on small sticky notes. Then they sort the ideas into categories. This is a great way to promote active listening and processing of reading content.

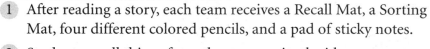

Activity Steps

1. After reading a story, each team receives a Recall Mat, a Sorting Mat, four different colored pencils, and a pad of sticky notes.

2. Students recall things from the story, write the idea or event on a sticky note, and announce it as they place the sticky note on the Recall Mat.

3. After students have numerous sticky notes on the Recall Mat, they pull out their Sorting Mat.

4. Teams discuss possible categories for their Sorting Mat. Once they reach consensus on the category names, they write them on the Sorting Mat.

5. Students take turns reading each sticky note and placing it on the Sorting Mat.

STRUCTURES

Jot Thoughts & Sorting

Blacklines

Recall Mat

Jot Thoughts

Instructions: Copy one mat per team. Use to generate ideas for Sorting Mat.

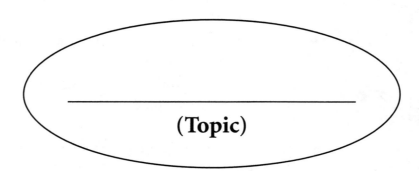

(Topic)

Sorting Mat

Jot Thoughts

Instructions: Copy one mat per team. Use to sort ideas from Recall Mat.

Idioms and Morals

Students discuss in teams the meaning of various idioms and fable morals in a fun and energizing format.

Activity Steps

1. Students form teams.

2. The teacher shares an idiom or fable moral by reading it and displaying it on the overhead.

3. Students individually write what it means.

4. Teammates stand at their team desk, put their heads together, and discuss what the statement means.

5. Students sit back down when ready.

6. The teacher calls a student number and says how many teams to move ahead.

7. The student called travels to the new team.

8. Students who rotated share their team's ideas with their new team.

9. The teacher then leads a group discussion of the statement's meaning.

10. The process is repeated for each new idiom or moral.

STRUCTURE

Traveling Heads Together

Blacklines

Idioms

Traveling Heads Together

Instructions: Teacher makes an overhead of this page and shares one idiom for each round of the activity.

- I would like **to be a fly on the wall** when he opens the gift.

- When the principal retired, the school had **big shoes to fill**.

- The winner of the contest was on **cloud nine**.

- The two cars passed within inches of each other. It was a **close shave**.

- The idea did not work out, but that's **how the cookie crumbles**.

- The youngest child was a **bottomless pit** at the dinner table.

- The expert's directions were **clear as mud**.

- We can't ask Matt and Sid to work **for peanuts**.

- The party was ruined when she **let the cat out of the bag** before the cake arrived.

- It was **raining cats and dogs** when we left for school.

Idioms

Traveling Heads Together

Instructions: Teacher makes an overhead of this page and shares one idiom for each round of the activity.

- The **early bird gets the worm** when we go shopping.

- Sue wished her pesky little sister would **go fly a kite**.

- The movie about space creatures made my **hair stand on end**.

- You can't **get your feet wet** by just watching others.

- When Tim started talking, he made **a mountain out of a molehill**.

- Your idea is working smoothly, so **don't rock the boat**.

- After looking over the papers, I **smelled a rat**.

- The two third grade friends were like **two peas in a pod**.

- The soccer team was losing, but they did not **throw in the towel**.

- Stop for a few minutes and **smell the roses**.

Idioms

Traveling Heads Together

Instructions: Teacher makes an overhead of this page and shares one idiom for each round of the activity.

- I have **a bone to pick** with you.

- Didn't Tom's idea **take the cake**?

- He went **out on a limb** for his best friend.

- When you make your plan, don't **put the cart before the horse**.

- When asked about what happened, she **passed the buck**.

- The basketball player was a **ball of fire** during the game.

- Mary was **barking up the wrong tree** when she asked Paul about the problem.

- When Tyler joined his third club, he **bit off more than he could chew**.

- After the model fell apart, we were **back to square one**.

- Jed loved all his children, but Polly was **the apple of his eye**.

Idioms

Traveling Heads Together

Instructions: Teacher makes an overhead of this page and shares one idiom for each round of the activity.

- Don't **beat around the bush**.

- That math problem was **easy as pie**.

- I could tell he was **all ears** during the speech.

- Sometimes it is a good idea to **hold one's tongue**.

- He passed the test by the **skin of his teeth**.

- After the team lost, she felt **down in the dumps**.

- Let's **grab a bite** before we go to the park.

- Sometimes it is hard to **keep one's chin up**.

- Pete decided to **let sleeping dogs lie**.

- We will be there **with bells on**.

- Pam decided to **hit the books** before the test.

Balanced Literacy • Third Grade • Skidmore & Graber
Kagan Publishing • 1 (800) 933-2667 • www.KaganOnline.com

Fable Morals
Traveling Heads Together

Instructions: Teacher makes an overhead of this page and shares one fable moral for each round of the activity.

- One good turn deserves another.

- A man is known by the company he keeps.

- Good things come in small packages.

- Beauty is in the eye of the beholder.

- Slow and steady wins the race.

- Appearance can be deceiving.

- Be careful what you wish for.

- Pride goes before a fall.

- Don't judge a book by its cover.

- No one likes a quitter.

- Biggest is not always best.

Fable Morals

Traveling Heads Together

Instructions: Teacher makes an overhead of this page and shares one fable moral for each round of the activity.

- It is sometimes better not to say anything.

- You can't please everyone all the time.

- Do not count your chickens before they hatch.

- Birds of a feather flock together.

- Look before you leap.

- Little friends may prove to be great friends.

- Honesty is the best policy.

- Fair weather friends are not worth much.

- He who is too greedy may end up with nothing.

- Kindness works better than force.

Idiom Meanings

Partners take turns matching idioms with their meanings.

STRUCTURE
RallyCoach

Activity Steps

1. Each pair receives an Idiom Mat and a set of Idiom Cards. (Two separate sets are provided.) They spread out the Idiom Cards so they can read them all.

2. Partner A chooses an idiom card (bold font) and a matching meaning card. Partner A places the cards across from each other in the correct columns on the Idiom Mat.

3. Partner B watches, listens, checks, and praises.

4. Partner B chooses an idiom card and a matching meaning card. Partner B places the cards across from each other in the correct columns on the Idiom Mat.

5. Partner A watches, listens, checks, and praises.

6. The process is continued until the pair fills out the Idiom Mat.

Blacklines

Idiom Mat
RallyCoach

Instructions: Copy for each pair of students.

Idiom	Meaning

Idiom Cards—Set 1 for Mat

RallyCoach

Instructions: Copy one set of cards for each pair of students. Cut apart.

Idiom Cards—Set 1	Idiom Cards—Set 1
as the crow flies	in a straight line between two points
Idiom Cards—Set 1	Idiom Cards—Set 1
at a snail's pace	very slowly
Idiom Cards—Set 1	Idiom Cards—Set 1
at the drop of a hat	quickly; with little notice
Idiom Cards—Set 1	Idiom Cards—Set 1
on the back burner	not urgent
Idiom Cards—Set 1	Idiom Cards—Set 1
ball of fire	a person who is full of energy
Idiom Cards—Set 1	Idiom Cards—Set 1
be a fly on the wall	to be an unseen observer
Idiom Cards—Set 1	Idiom Cards—Set 1
blow one's stack	to show sudden, explosive anger
Idiom Cards—Set 1	Idiom Cards—Set 1
catch a wink	fall asleep for a short time
Idiom Cards—Set 1	Idiom Cards—Set 1
close shave	an experience that was dangerous
Idiom Cards—Set 1	Idiom Cards—Set 1
cloud nine	state of extreme excitement and happiness

Idiom Cards—Set 2 for Mat

RallyCoach

Instructions: Copy one set of cards for each pair of students. Cut apart.

Idiom Cards — Set 2	Idiom Cards — Set 2
eat like a bird	to eat very little
Idiom Cards — Set 2	Idiom Cards — Set 2
eat like a horse	to eat a large amount
Idiom Cards — Set 2	Idiom Cards — Set 2
feel blue	experience sadness
Idiom Cards — Set 2	Idiom Cards — Set 2
foot the bill	pay the charges
Idiom Cards — Set 2	Idiom Cards — Set 2
go fly a kite	to go away
Idiom Cards — Set 2	Idiom Cards — Set 2
hit the books	to study hard
Idiom Cards — Set 2	Idiom Cards — Set 2
hit the hay	to go to bed
Idiom Cards — Set 2	Idiom Cards — Set 2
pick up the tab	to pay the bill
Idiom Cards — Set 2	Idiom Cards — Set 2
raining cats and dogs	raining heavily
Idiom Cards — Set 2	Idiom Cards — Set 2
smell the roses	enjoy life

Sequencing Events

Teammates each receive a card with an event on it, and they position themselves in a line so that they correctly sequence the event.

STRUCTURE

Team Line-Ups

Activity Steps

1. Each team receives one set of Sequencing Event Cards. (Six different sets are provided.) Each student gets one card.

2. Each teammate reads his/her card using RoundRobin.

3. Student #1 states where he/she should stand in the team line-up and gets consensus from teammates (thumbs up).

4. Students #2–4 repeat Step 3.

5. Team checks the finished sequence, makes adjustments if necessary, and celebrates when correct.

Blacklines

Sequencing Events Cards
Team Line-Ups

Instructions: Copy one set of cards for each team. Cut apart.

The Butterfly

Sequencing Event Cards—Set 1
The Butterfly

The caterpillar ate and ate and ate.

Sequencing Event Cards—Set 1
The Butterfly

He attached himself to a branch and made a chrysalis.

Sequencing Event Cards—Set 1
The Butterfly

The caterpillar became very fat.

Sequencing Event Cards—Set 1
The Butterfly

After two weeks, a beautiful butterfly emerged.

The Fire

Sequencing Event Cards—Set 2
The Fire

We gathered some logs and put them in a pile.

Sequencing Event Cards—Set 2
The Fire

The flame from a match lit a newspaper.

Sequencing Event Cards—Set 2
The Fire

Dry leaves and newspapers were placed in between the logs.

Sequencing Event Cards—Set 2
The Fire

The flames began to burn the logs.

Sequencing Events Cards
Team Line-Ups

Instructions: Copy one set of cards for each team. Cut apart.

Bubble Gum

Sequencing Event Cards—Set 3 **Bubble Gum**	Sequencing Event Cards—Set 3 **Bubble Gum**
Chew, chew, chew!	With your lips on top of your tongue, blow air into the gum.

Sequencing Event Cards—Set 3 **Bubble Gum**	Sequencing Event Cards—Set 3 **Bubble Gum**
Wrap the gum around your tongue.	A huge bubble will begin to grow.

After School

Sequencing Event Cards—Set 4 **After School**	Sequencing Event Cards—Set 4 **After School**
I came home from school at 4:00.	By 4:30 my homework was finished.

Sequencing Event Cards—Set 4 **After School**	Sequencing Event Cards—Set 4 **After School**
At 4:15 I ate my snack.	I played outside until 5:30.

Sequencing Events Cards
Team Line-Ups

Instructions: Copy one set of cards for each team. Cut apart.

The Bee

<table>
<tr>
<td>

Sequencing Event Cards—Set 5
The Bee

The bee buzzed
around the flower.

</td>
<td>

Sequencing Event Cards—Set 5
The Bee

Soon the bee flew to
another flower.

</td>
</tr>
<tr>
<td>

Sequencing Event Cards—Set 5
The Bee

The bee landed in the center
of a red flower.

</td>
<td>

Sequencing Event Cards—Set 5
The Bee

The bee took off for
its hive.

</td>
</tr>
</table>

Brushing Teeth

<table>
<tr>
<td>

Sequencing Event Cards—Set 6
Brushing Teeth

Get your toothbrush
and toothpaste.

</td>
<td>

Sequencing Event Cards—Set 6
Brushing Teeth

Move your brush around in
your mouth.

</td>
</tr>
<tr>
<td>

Sequencing Event Cards—Set 6
Brushing Teeth

Make your toothbrush wet with
water and squeeze toothpaste
on your toothbrush.

</td>
<td>

Sequencing Event Cards—Set 6
Brushing Teeth

Spit out toothpaste.

</td>
</tr>
</table>

Word Study

Word Study

Effective word study instruction involves both decoding words and deriving meaning from words (vocabulary). Word study allows students to take words apart while reading and put word parts together while writing. Word-solving strategies help students learn important concepts related to decoding, spelling, and understanding vocabulary. As students participate in word study activities, they become aware of relationships between sounds, letters, letter combinations, and word parts. Various cooperative activities in this book provide opportunities for students to practice application of word study skills and decoding strategies for effective reading and writing.

Following the framework of balanced literacy allows the teacher to scaffold instruction through use of explicit teaching during read/write alouds and shared reading/writing to explain strategies used to decode words and understand their meanings. Scaffolding continues during guided reading/writing as the teacher monitors and provides feedback to students applying word-solving skills and strategies. Support is withdrawn as students independently apply these skills and strategies successfully.

Table of Word Study Resources

Page(s)	Resources	Balanced Literacy				
		Aloud	Shared	Guided	Independent	Literature Circles
	Word Study Descriptions and Lists					
178	Word Study Resources/ Materials Descriptions					
179	Spelling Strategies	●	●	●	●	●
180	Prefix and Suffix Word List	●	●	●	●	●
181	Contractions List	●	●	●	●	●
182	Homophone List	●	●	●	●	●
185	Compound Word List	●	●	●	●	●

Table of Word Study Activities and Lessons

Page(s)	Activities/Lessons	Blacklines	Balanced Literacy				
			Aloud	Shared	Guided	Independent	Literature Circles
196	Partner Word Study Activities		●	●	●	●	●
200	Team Word Study Actitivites		●	●	●	●	●
204	Classs Word Study Actitivites		●	●	●	●	●
205	**Making Words Lesson Plans**						
206	**Lesson 1: "Weather"**						
206	**RallyCoach Activity**						
206	Activity 1: Making Words	• Teacher Tranparency Form • Student Form	●	●	●	●	
208	**Find My Rule Activity**						
208	Activity 2: Sorting	• Teacher Tranparency Form • Find My Rule Mat	●	●	●	●	
209	**RallyCoach Activity**						
209	Activity 3: Transfer		●	●	●	●	
212	**Lesson 2: "Cereals"**						
212	**RallyCoach Activity**						
212	Activity 1: Making Words	• Teacher Tranparency Form • Student Form	●	●	●	●	
213	**Find My Rule Activity**						
213	Activity 2: Sorting	• Teacher Tranparency Form • Find My Rule Mat	●	●	●	●	
213	**RallyCoach Activity**						
213	Activity 3: Transfer		●	●	●	●	

Balanced Literacy • Third Grade • Skidmore & Graber
Kagan Publishing • 1 (800) 933-2667 • www.KaganOnline.com

Table of Word Study Activities and Lessons (continued)

Page(s)	Activities/Lessons	Resources	Balanced Literacy				
			Aloud	Shared	Guided	Independent	Literature Circles
216	**Lesson 3: "Permanent"**						
216	**RallyCoach Activity**						
216	Activity 1: Making Words	• Teacher Tranparency Form • Student Form	●	●	●	●	
217	**Find My Rule Activity**						
217	Activity 2: Sorting	• Teacher Tranparency Form • Find My Rule Mat	●	●	●	●	
217	**RallyCoach Activity**						
217	Activity 3: Transfer						
223	**Find Someone Who Activity — Who Knows?**						
224	All About Contractions!	• Worksheet		●	●		
225	All About ur, ir, er	• Worksheet		●	●		
226	All About Compound Words!	• Worksheet		●	●		
227	Skill Review	• Worksheet		●	●		
228	Find Someone Who	• Form		●	●		
229	**Quiz-Quiz-Trade Activity — Partner Word Study Practice**						
230	Antonyms	• Question/Answer Cards					
237	Synonyms	• Question/Answer Cards		●	●		
244	Contractions	• Question/Answer Cards		●	●		
250	Prefixes (mis-, pre-)	• Question/Answer Cards		●	●		
259	Letter Patterns (oi, oy)	• Question/Answer Cards		●	●		
266	Letter Patterns (au, aw)	• Question/Answer Cards		●	●		
273	Letter Patterns (ou, ow)	• Question/Answer Cards		●	●		

Table of Word Study Activities and Lessons (continued)

Page(s)	Activities/Lessons	Blacklines	Balanced Literacy				
			Aloud	Shared	Guided	Independent	Literature Circles
280	**RallyCoach Activity — Coach Me**						
281	Prefixes (mis- and pre-)	• Cube • Worksheet		●	●		
283	Suffixes (-less and -ness)	• Cube • Worksheet		●	●		
285	Antonyms and Synonyms	• Cube • Worksheet		●	●		
287	er, ir, ur	• Spinner • Worksheet		●	●		
289	Contractions	• Spinner • Worksheet		●	●		
291	Forming Plurals	• Spinner • Worksheet		●	●		
293	Adding s, es	• Sorting Mat Word Cards		●	●		
297	Hard c, Soft c	• Sorting Mat Word Cards		●	●		
302	Words with ea	• Sorting Mat Word Cards		●	●		
306	Rare Singulars and Plurals	• Sorting Mat Word Cards		●	●		
308	**Showdown Activity — Word Study**						
309	Prefixes (mis-, pre-)	• Cards		●	●		
312	Suffixes (-less, -ness)	• Cards		●	●		
315	Antonyms, Synonyms, Homophones	• Cards		●	●		
323	**Numbered Heads Together Activity — Word Wall Spelling**						
324	Word Wall Words	• Priority Word List • Priority Word Wall Cards • Blank Word Wall Cards	●	●			

Balanced Literacy • Third Grade • Skidmore & Graber
Kagan Publishing • 1 (800) 933-2667 • www.KaganOnline.com

Word Study
Resources

Word Study Resource Descriptions

Resources/Materials Descriptions

Spelling Strategies (p. 179)
The goal of word study is to spell words correctly in everyday writing. Spelling strategies, which students should learn to use, are listed as a resource. Several of the Kagan activities in this book reinforce these spelling strategies.

Prefix and Suffix Word List (p. 180)
This resource lists several prefixes and suffixes, their meanings, and word examples.

Contractions List (p. 181)
This contraction list includes contractions made with *am, are, had, would, have, is, has, not, us,* and *will.*

Homophone List (p. 182)
Homophones are words that are spelled differently, but sound the same such as *rain, rein, reign.* This homophone list is a classroom resource for teachers and students.

Compound Word List (p. 185)
Compound words are made by combining two words. This compound word list is a resource for teachers and students.

Word Study Activities (p. 196)
These word study activities are arranged according to partner, team, and class activities. The Kagan cooperative learning structure, activity name, and a brief description are included.

Balanced Literacy • Third Grade • Skidmore & Graber
Kagan Publishing • 1 (800) 933-2667 • www.KaganOnline.com

Word Study Spelling Strategies

Visualize it.  Word	**Try it several ways. Which way looks right?**
Stretch it out. Listen to the sounds. · Letter patterns · Endings · Prefixes	**Ask a friend.**
Circle the word. Come back later.  Word	**Check the Word Wall.** 
Use what you already know. (analogy)  Blue ➔ Glue	**Use a dictionary or spell check.** 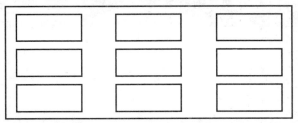

Word Study Prefix and Suffix Word List

Teacher Resources

Prefixes		
mis–	"wrongly"	mistake, mislead, miscount, misdeed, misunderstood, misprint, miscue, mishap, mismatch, misinform, misinterpret, mispronounce, misfortune, misfit, misgiving, misbehave, misplace, miscalculate, misspell, misfire, mishandle, misread, misdirect
pre–	"before, prior to"	preheat, prehistoric, pretest, preschool, precaution, prepay, prepaid, predate, prefix, preserve, preview, precook, precondition, prearrange, prejudge

Suffixes		
–less	"without"	motherless, careless, ageless, useless, harmless, aimless, blameless, boneless, endless, priceless, scoreless, tasteless, timeless, wireless, painless, needless, pointless, helpless, bottomless, breathless, stainless, reckless, worthless, thankless, soundless, lifeless, speechless, sleepless, homeless, spotless, cheerless, hairless, sightless, shapeless, mindless
–ness	"state of being"	happiness, loudness, sickness, goodness, darkness, kindness, willingness, sadness, tenderness, usefulness, carefulness, heaviness, suddenness, toughness

Word Study Contractions List

am
I'm

are
they're
we're
you're

had would
I'd
it'd
she'd
there'd
they'd

have
could've
I've
might've
should've
they've
we've
would've
you've

is has
here's
he's
it's
she's
that's
there's
what's
where's

not
aren't
can't
couldn't
didn't
doesn't
don't
hadn't
hasn't
haven't
isn't
mustn't
needn't
shouldn't
wouldn't

us
let's

will
I'll
it'll
he'll
she'll
that'll
they'll
we'll
you'll

Word Study Homophone List

accept/except	bough/bow	creak/creek	genes/jeans
ad/add	boy/buoy	cymbal/symbol	great/grate
affect/effect	break/brake	days/daze	groan/grown
ail/ale	brews/bruise	dear/deer	guessed/guest
aisle/I'll/isle	bridal/bridle	dew/do/due	hail/hale
all/awl	buy/by/bye	die/dye	hall/haul
aloud/allowed	capital/capitol	doe/dough	hare/hair
alter/altar	carat/caret/carrot	dual/duel	hay/hey
ant/aunt	caught/cot	earn/urn	heal/heel/he'll
arc/ark	ceiling/sealing	ewe/yew/you	hear/here
ate/eight	cell/sell	eye/I	heard/herd
aye/eye/I	cellar/seller	fair/fare	hi/high
bale/bail	cent/sent/scent	fairy/ferry	higher/hire
ball/bawl	cents/scents/sense	feat/feet	him/hymn
base/bass	cereal/serial	find/fined	hoarse/horse
be/bee	cheap/cheep	fir/fur	hole/whole
bear/bare	chews/choose	flair/flare	holy/wholly
beat/beet	chili/chilly	flea/flee	hour/our
beau/bow	choral/coral	flew/flue/flue	idle/idol
berry/bury	chord/cord	flour/flower	in/inn
billed/build	chute/shoot	foaled/fold	Jim/gym
bite/byte	cite/sight/site	for/fore/four	knead/need
blue/blew	close/clothes	foreword/forward	knew/new
boar/bore	coarse/course	forth/fourth	knight/night
board/bored	core/corps	foul/fowl	knit/nit
bold/bowled	council/counsel	gate/gait	knot/not

Word Study
Homophone List
(continued)

know/no	pair/pare/pear	red/read	
knows/nose	past/passed	right/rite/write	
lead/led	patience/patients	ring/wring	
leak/leek	pause/paws	road/rode/rowed	
lessen/lesson	peace/piece	role/roll	
lie/lye	peal/peel	root/route	
links/lynx	pearl/purl	rose/rows	
load/lode	pedal/peddle	rote/wrote	
loot/lute	peek/peak	rough/ruff	
made/maid	peer/pier	rye/wry	
mail/male	pi/pie	sail/sale	
main/Maine/mane	plane/plain	scene/seen	
Mary/marry/merry	plum/plumb	sea/see	
meat/meet	pole/poll	seam/seam	
might/mite	pour/pore	sew/so/sow	
mind/mined	praise/prays/preys	shear/sheer	
missed/mist	pray/prey	shoe/shoo	
moose/mousse	presence/presents	shone/shown	
none/nun	prince/prints	side/sighed	
oar/or/ore	principal/principle	sole/soul	
oh/owe	profit/prophet	some/sum	
one/won	quarts/quartz	son/sun	
overdo/overdue	rain/reign/rein	stair/stare	
paced/paste	raise/rays/raze	stake/steak	
pail/pale	rap/wrap	stationary/stationery	
pain/pane	real/reel	steal/steel	

Word Study
Homophone List
(continued)

straight/strait	wait/weight		
suite/sweet	waive/wave		
sundae/Sunday	ware/wear/where		
tacks/tax	wave/waive		
tail/tale	way/weigh/whey		
tea/tee	we/wee		
team/teem	weak/week		
teas/tease/tees	weather/whether		
their/there/they're	weave/we've		
theirs/there's	we'd/weed		
threw/through	were/whirr		
throne/thrown	which/witch		
thyme/time	whine/wine		
tide/tied	who's/whose		
to/too/two	woe/whoa		
toad/towed	wood/would		
told/tolled	worn/warn		
tow/toe	yoke/yolk		
troop/troupe	you/ewe		
vain/vane/vein	you'll/Yule		
vale/veil	your/you're		
vary/very			
vial/vile			
wade/weighed			
wail/whale			
waist/waste			

Word Study Compound Word List

aircraft	bedroom	butterfingers	corkscrew
airplane	bedspread	butterfly	cornerstone
airport	bedtime	buttermilk	cornstalk
anybody	beeline	campfire	cornstarch
anyone	bellhop	cannot	cottontail
anyplace	billboard	capsize	cottonwood
anything	birdhouse	carhop	countdown
anywhere	birthday	catfish	courthouse
applesauce	blacktop	catnip	courtyard
armchair	blockbuster	cattail	cowboy
arrowhead	bobcat	chalkboard	cowgirl
audiotape	bobtail	championship	cowpoke
backfire	bookmobile	checkmate	crabgrass
background	boxcar	checkup	crackerjack
backstroke	boyfriend	cheesecloth	crossbar
backtrack	brainstorm	chestnut	crossbones
backyard	brainwash	chopstick	crosscurrent
bagpipe	briefcase	citizenship	crossroad
ballroom	broadcast	classmate	crosswalk
bankroll	brotherhood	clockwise	crowbar
barefoot	bucktooth	clockwork	crybaby
barnyard	bulldog	cobweb	cubbyhole
baseball	bulldozer	cockpit	cupboard
bathroom	bullfrog	cookbook	cupcake
beachcomber	bullheaded	copycat	cutback
bedroll	buttercup	copyright	daredevil

Word Study
Compound Word List
(continued)

darkroom	dropkick	fairway	floodgate
dashboard	drugstore	falsehood	floodlight
daybreak	drumstick	fanfare	flycatcher
daydream	dugout	farewell	flypaper
daylight	dustpan	farmhouse	foghorn
daytime	earache	farmyard	folklore
deadline	earmuff	featherbed	folktale
dishwasher	earring	featherweight	foolproof
dogcatcher	earshot	feedback	football
dogsled	earthquake	fellowship	foothill
doorbell	eggplant	fiddlesticks	foothold
doorknob	elbowroom	fingernail	footlights
doormat	elsewhere	firecracker	footlocker
doorway	evergreen	firefighter	footnote
doughnut	everybody	firefly	footpath
downhill	everyone	fireproof	footprint
downpour	everything	firewood	footrest
downstairs	everywhere	fishbowl	footstep
downstream	eyeball	fisherman	footstool
downtown	eyebrow	fishhook	forecast
downwind	eyelash	flagpole	forefather
drainpipe	eyelid	flapjack	foreground
drawbridge	eyesight	flashback	foreman
drawstring	eyesore	flashlight	forenoon
dressmaker	eyestrain	flatcar	foresight
driveway	eyewitness	flatfoot	forever

Word Study
Compound Word List
(continued)

fourteen	grandstand	handball	headphone
foxhole	grapefruit	handbook	headquarters
framework	grapevine	handcuff	headrest
freehand	grasshopper	handmade	headwaiter
freeman	grassland	handout	hearsay
freeway	gravestone	handsome	heartache
freshman	graveyard	handwriting	heartbreak
freshwater	greyhound	handyman	heartburn
frostbite	griddlecake	hangout	heartsick
fullback	groundwork	hardship	heavyset
gangplank	guardhouse	hardware	heavyweight
gatekeeper	guesswork	hardwood	hedgehog
girlfriend	guidebook	hayfork	heirloom
giveaway	guideline	hayloft	herself
globetrotter	guidepost	haystack	heyday
goalkeeper	gumdrop	haywire	hideaway
goldfish	hailstone	hazelnut	highlands
goldsmith	hairbrush	headache	highlight
gooseberry	haircut	headband	highway
grandchildren	hairdo	headdress	hillbilly
granddaughter	hairdresser	headfirst	hillside
grandfather	hairline	headgear	hilltop
grandma	halfback	headlight	himself
grandmother	halfway	headline	hindsight
grandpa	hamburger	headmaster	hoedown
grandson	handbag	headmistress	hogwash

Word Study
Compound Word List
(continued)

hollyhock	housefly	jitterbug	letterhead
Hollywood	household	johnnycake	lifeboat
homebody	housekeeper	keepsake	lifeguard
homecoming	housewarming	keyboard	lifelong
homeland	housework	keyhole	lifetime
homemade	humankind	keynote	lightheaded
homeroom	humbug	kickoff	lighthouse
homesick	humdinger	kickstand	lightweight
homestead	hummingbird	kindhearted	likewise
homework	humpback	knapsack	limelight
honeybee	iceberg	kneecap	limestone
honeycomb	iccebox	knockout	lineman
honeydew	icebreaker	knothole	lipstick
honeymoon	inchworm	ladybug	litterbug
hookup	indoors	ladyfinger	livestock
hopscotch	infield	landholder	lockout
horseback	inkblot	landlord	logrolling
horsefly	inside	landmark	lookout
horseplay	into	landslide	loophole
horsepower	itself	lawmaker	lopsided
horseradish	jackpot	lawsuit	loudmouth
horseshoe	jawbone	layoff	lovebird
hotheaded	jawbreaker	layout	lukewarm
hourglass	jaywalk	layover	lumberjack
houseboat	jellyfish	leapfrog	lumberyard
housecoat	jigsaw	leftovers	mailbox

 Balanced Literacy • Third Grade • Skidmore & Graber
Kagan Publishing • 1 (800) 933-2667 • www.KaganOnline.com

Word Study
Compound Word List
(continued)

mailman	moonshine	nobody	outside
mainland	motorcycle	noonday	overact
mainstream	mousetrap	noontime	overactive
makeshift	mouthpiece	notebook	overall
manhole	mouthwash	noteworthy	overcoat
mankind	muskrat	nutcracker	overexcite
manpower	myself	nuthatch	overexert
marketplace	namesake	nutshell	overextend
markup	neckline	offbeat	overfeed
masterpiece	needlepoint	offshore	overfill
matchbook	neighborhood	offspring	overflow
matchmaker	network	oncoming	overgrown
maybe	newborn	oneself	overhand
mayflower	newcomer	ongoing	overhaul
maypole	newsboy	onlooker	overhead
mealtime	newscast	otherwise	overhear
meanwhile	newsletter	ourselves	overheat
merrymaking	newspaper	outbid	overjoyed
milkman	newsprint	outburst	overnight
milkweed	necktie	outcry	overpass
millstream	nightcap	outdistance	overpay
minuteman	nightclothes	outdoors	overpopulate
mockingbird	nightgown	outfield	overripe
molehill	nightmare	outfit	overrun
monkeyshine	nightstick	outgoing	overseas
moonlight	nighttime	outsell	oversee

Word Study
Compound Word List
(continued)

oversize	pigeonhole	potpie	ripcord
oversleep	piggyback	powerboat	riverside
overstuffed	pigpen	powerhouse	roadrunner
overtake	pigtail	praiseworthy	roadside
overthrow	pillbox	pressroom	roadway
overtime	pillowcase	proofread	rollerblade
overuse	pincushion	pullover	roommate
pacemaker	pineapple	pushcart	rosebud
pancake	pinhole	quarterback	roughneck
paperback	pinkeye	quicksand	roundabout
paperwork	pinpoint	racehorse	roundup
parkway	pinstripe	racetrack	rowboat
passport	pinwheel	ragtime	runaway
password	pipeline	ragweed	runoff
patchwork	plainclothes	railroad	safeguard
pathfinder	playground	railway	safekeeping
pathway	playhouse	rainbow	sagebrush
payoff	playpen	raincoat	sailboat
payroll	plaything	rainfall	salesperson
peacemaker	pocketbook	rainstorm	saltshaker
peanut	policeman	rainwater	saltwater
peephole	popcorn	rattlesnake	sandalwood
penlight	potbelly	redhead	sandbar
pitchfork	potholder	redwood	sandblast
pickax	pothole	ringleader	sandbox
pickup	potluck	ringworm	sandman

Word Study
Compound Word List
(continued)

sandpaper	shellfish	sightseeing	snowflake
sandstone	shipbuilding	silkworm	snowman
sandstorm	shipshape	silversmith	snowplow
saucepan	shipwreck	silverware	snoeshoes
sawdust	shipyard	singsong	snowstorm
scarecrow	shoelace	skylark	softball
scatterbrain	shoemaker	skylight	somebody
schoolboy	shopkeeper	skyline	someday
schoolgirl	shopwindow	skyrocket	somehow
schoolhouse	shorebird	skyscraper	someone
schoolteacher	shoreline	skywriting	someplace
scrapbook	shortcake	slapstick	something
screenplay	shortcoming	sleepwalking	sometime
screwdriver	shortsighted	sleepyhead	someway
seaboard	shortstop	slingshot	somewhat
seacoast	showcase	slipcover	somewhere
seafood	showoff	slipknot	songbird
searchlight	shuffleboard	smallpox	soundproof
seashell	sickbed	smokehouse	soundtrack
seashore	sideburns	smokestack	sourpuss
seasick	sidecar	snapdragon	southeast
secondhand	sidekick	snapshot	soybean
sendoff	sidesaddle	snowball	spacecraft
setback	sidestep	snowbound	spaceship
sharecropper	sidestroke	snowdrift	speedway
sheepskin	sideway	snowfall	spellbound

Word Study
Compound Word List
(continued)

spendthrift	stepson	sunroom	textbook
spillway	stockpile	sunset	thanksgiving
sportswear	stopwatch	sunshine	themselves
spotlight	storehouse	sunspot	thoroughbred
springboard	storekeeper	sunstroke	threadbare
springtime	storeroom	suntan	throughout
spyglass	stovepipe	superhuman	thumbtack
stagecoach	stowaway	superman	thunderbird
staircase	straightedge	supermarket	thunderbolt
stairway	strawberry	surfboard	thunderclap
standby	streetcar	swallowtail	thundercloud
standstill	strikeout	sweepstakes	thunderstorm
starfish	stronghold	sweetheart	tidewater
starlight	sugarplum	switchboard	tightlipped
steadfast	suitcase	swordfish	tightrope
steamboat	summertime	tablecloth	timberline
steamroller	sunburn	tablespoon	timekeeper
stepbrother	Sunday	taillight	timepiece
stepchild	sundial	takeoff	timetable
stepdaughter	sundown	taproot	timeworn
stepfather	sunfish	tattletale	tinfoil
stepladder	sunflower	teammate	tiptoe
stepmother	sunglasses	teardrop	toadstool
stepparent	sunlight	teaspoon	today
steppingstone	sunlit	tenderloin	toenail
stepsister	sunrise	tenpin	tollgate

 Balanced Literacy • Third Grade • Skidmore & Graber
Kagan Publishing • 1 (800) 933-2667 • www.KaganOnline.com

Word Study
Compound Word List
(continued)

tomboy	underbrush	underweight	warlike
tombstone	undercharge	upbeat	warpath
tomcat	undercoat	upbringing	wartime
toothbrush	undercook	upcoming	washboard
toothpaste	undercover	update	washcloth
toothpick	undercurrent	upgrade	washroom
topcoat	underdeveloped	uphill	washtub
tossup	underdog	upkeep	wasteland
touchdown	underfed	uplift	watchdog
townspeople	underfoot	upon	watchman
trademark	underground	upright	waterfall
treadmill	underline	uproar	waterfowl
troublemaker	undernourished	uproot	waterfront
truckload	underpass	upset	watermelon
trustworthy	underpay	upstairs	waterproof
tryout	underprivileged	upstream	watershed
tugboat	undershirt	uptown	waterspout
tumbleweed	underside	videotape	waterway
turnabout	undersized	viewpoint	wavelength
turnover	understaffed	vineyard	wayside
turnpike	understand	volleyball	weatherman
turntable	understood	waistline	weatherproof
turtledove	undertaker	wallpaper	weekday
typewriter	undertow	wardrobe	weekend
underachieve	underwater	warehouse	weightlifting
underarm	underwear	warfare	whatever

Word Study
Compound Word List
(continued)

wheelchair	within		
whenever	without		
whichever	wonderland		
whirlpool	woodcarving		
whiteboard	woodchuck		
wholesale	woodcutter		
wholesome	woodland		
widespread	woodpecker		
wildcat	woodwork		
wildfire	workbench		
wildlife	workout		
windburn	workroom		
windmill	workshop		
windowpane	worldwide		
windowsill	worthwhile		
windshield	yardstick		
windsock	yearbook		
windstorm	yourself		
wingspan			
wintergreen			
wintertime			
wiretap			
wisecrack			
wishbone			
withdraw			
withhold			

Balanced Literacy • Third Grade • Skidmore & Graber
Kagan Publishing • 1 (800) 933-2667 • www.KaganOnline.com

Word Study Activities and Lessons

Partner Word Study Activities

Match My Word

Structure: Match Mine

Use stand-up folders as buddy barriers. The teacher shows Partner A a slip of paper with a word study word on it. Partner A writes the word on a small dry-erase board, which Partner B cannot see. Partner A tells Partner B how to spell the word on his or her dry-erase board. The directions may include how to form the letters, but the letter names may not be said. Partners switch roles for the next word.

Big Words/Little Words

Structure: RallyCoach

The teacher makes individual letter cards for words. These are packaged in separate bags. Partners take a bag and take turns making as many different words as they can using the letters from the bag. Each word is recorded. A mystery word can be made by using all the letters in the bag.

Computer Typing

Structure: RallyCoach

Partners use a word list to take turns giving each other words to type on a word-processing program on the computer. They change the font style and sizes, so each word looks different. Print out the words to see the finished product.

Foamy Fun

Structure: RallyCoach

Partners sit side by side. The teacher squirts a heap of shaving cream on a protected surface. One at a time, the teacher calls out the word study words. The partners use their fingertips to write the word in the foam. Partners check and praise each other.

Hand Spelling

Structure: RallyCoach

Partner A traces the letters of a word in the palm of Partner B's hand. Partner A says the name of the traced word. Partners take turns tracing the word, praising, coaching, and naming the word. Partners try identifying the word while looking and then with eyes closed.

Illustrating Words

Structure: RallyCoach

Partners take turns giving each other a word from a list. Partner A gives Partner B a word. Partner B writes the word and draws a picture to represent the word. Partner B then explains the picture and spells the word aloud without looking. Partner A praises and coaches. Partner B then gives a word to Partner A. Each word has its own box on the paper.

Partner Word Study Activities
(continued)

Inflatable Ball Spelling

Structure: RallyCoach

Use an inflatable ball with letters printed on it. (You may purchase one with letters already on it or make your own by printing letters with a permanent marker.) Partners take turns tossing the ball back and forth. When the catcher gets the ball, he or she lifts one hand and sees which letter is under it. As quickly as possible, he or she says a word beginning with that letter and spells it. Together partners decide if the word is correctly spelled and record it on paper.

Letter Ladders

Structure: RallyCoach

Partners are given a set of letter cards (one of every consonant and several of every vowel). Partners take turns making new words by changing one letter at a time. The teacher begins by giving the first word (for example, *hat*). Partner A may change the *h* to *c* to make a new word (*cat*) above the first word. Partner B may then change the *t* to *n* to make can. Challenge partners to see how tall they can make their ladders.

Memory

Structure: RallyCoach

Partners work together to make two identical word cards for each word on the list. Partners check each other's word cards. The cards are mixed up and placed facedown in rows. Partner A turns over two cards, saying the words. If the cards are a match, he or she removes them, spells the word without looking, and takes another turn. If they are not a match, the cards are turned facedown, and Partner B has a turn. Partners praise and coach each other.

Onsets and Rimes

Structure: RallyCoach

Partners use a container filled with individual onsets. They take turns adding these to rimes provided by the teacher to make new words, which are recorded on paper. Partners check then coach or praise.

On My Back

Structure: RallyCoach

Partner A sits on a chair without a back. Partner B stands in back with a list of words. Partner B "draws" the letters to spell a word on the back of Partner A. Partner A writes the word on paper. Partner B praises and coaches. Partners switch roles.

Partner Word Study Activities
(continued)

Roll a Word

Structure: RallyCoach

Prepare two large dice by writing onsets on one and rimes on the other. Partners take turns rolling both dice. If a word is rolled, partners praise and both write the word. If the roll does not make a word, the partner rolls the dice again until a word is rolled.

Sit and Spell

Structure: RallyCoach

The teacher writes a word list on the chalkboard. Students sit in two lines facing one another, so that only one line of students can see the word list. Students identify their partners, who are directly across from them. Partners A, who can see the words, are the "callers." Partners B are the "spellers." A caller reads a word aloud and listens carefully as the partner spells the word. If an incorrect spelling is given, the caller repeats the word and the partners spell it together. If a correct spelling is given, the partner praises. Partners switch roles for the next word.

Spelling Takes a Hit

Structure: RallyCoach

Partner A gives Partner B a word to spell by using a flyswatter to "hit" letters printed on a shower curtain hung on a wall. Partner A praises and coaches. Partners take turns giving the word and "hitting" the letters.

Study Buddies

Structure: RallyCoach

Partners take turns giving each other words to spell. A form with three columns is used. Partner A gives a word to Partner B to write in the first column. If the word is spelled correctly the first time, Partner A gives another word, which is written in a new first column. If the word is not spelled correctly, Partner B tries again in the second column. If that word is not correct, Partner A coaches by showing the word. Partner B writes it again in the third column. At any point that the word is correctly spelled, the partner is given a smiley face by the word. Partners switch roles when the words on the list have been spelled correctly or when the teacher indicates it is time to switch roles.

Water Spelling

Structure: RallyCoach

Partner A gives Partner B a word to spell on the sidewalk using a paintbrush and a container of water. Partner A praises and coaches. Partners take turns giving the word and "painting" it. (Note: Water sticks—plastic tubes with sponges on the ends—may also be used to "paint" words on the chalkboard.)

Partner Word Study Activities

(continued)

Word Search

Structure: RallyCoach

Students use graph paper to create their own word searches, including the words they are focusing on for that week. Students form partners. Using one partner's word search, partners take turns circling one hidden word at a time. Each partner has a different colored pencil. Partners coach and praise. When one word search is completed, the other one is used.

Tic-Tac-Toe—Three Words in a Row

Structure: RallyRobin

Each set of partners is given a set of word cards, a Tic-Tac-Toe worksheet, and two different colors or types of counters. Partner A picks up a card and reads it to Partner B. If Partner B correctly spells the word, he or she places a counter on any open square of the game board. If Partner B gives an incorrect response, Partner A correctly spells the word and coaches Partner B to spell the word correctly. The word card is placed at the bottom of the pile and no counter is placed on the game board. Partner A now has a turn to spell the next word. Partners try to place three counters in a row (horizontally, vertically, or diagonally). Partners celebrate.

Word Family Race

Structure: RallyTable

Partners have a letter die and a sheet of paper. Partner A rolls the die and announces the letter it lands on. Together the partners decide on a word that begins with that letter. For example, if the die lands on the letter *c*, the word *cat* could be written. Partners then take turns writing words in the word family. For example, Partner A could write *mat*. Partner B could write *flat*. Partners continue to alternate generating written words. When neither partner can think of another word belonging in the word family, the letter die is rolled again and new words are generated.

Spelling Toss

Structure: RallyToss

Partners spell a word while tossing a ball back and forth. Each partner says the next letter of the word until the word is spelled.

Word Toss Game

Structure: RallyToss

Partner A tosses a ball to Partner B at the same time as saying a word. Partner B writes the word on paper and spells it aloud to Partner A. Partner A praises or coaches. Continue by switching roles.

Team Word Study Activities

Spelling Detective

Structure: CenterPiece

Each team needs a page from a newspaper for each teammember and one for the center. Each teammember has a different colored pencil. The teacher calls out a word pattern and students look for a word on their newspaper page, which fits the pattern, and circle it. Students then trade their paper with the one in the center. Students continue circling words which fit the pattern until the teacher calls a new word pattern (examples: silent *e*, -ing ending, end chunk, etc.).

Add On Relay

Structure: RoundTable

A team forms a line facing the chalkboard. Teammate #1 gives a word. Teammate #2 goes to the chalkboard and writes the first letter of the word, returning to the line and handing the chalk to Teammate #3, who writes the second letter of the word. Continue in this manner, until the word is spelled. If a student sees that a team member has made a spelling error, he or she may use a turn to correct the error. Teammate #2 gives the second word. (A markerboard could also be used.)

Scrambled Word Problem Solving

Structure: Jigsaw Problem Solving

Each team is given a bag with the individual letters of a word. Teammates each take a letter or letters, until all the letters are taken. Student #1 states his or her letter and where it goes in the sequence. Teammates check, coach, and move letters. Process continues with each teammate until word is spelled correctly. When the word is spelled correctly, the team receives a new bag with a new word.

Bean Bag Word Family Game

Structure: RoundTable

Each team needs a set of laminated cards with a word family written on the top (for example: ind, ant, ine), a set of word cards, a beanbag, and a different colored transparency pen for each student. Lay out the set of word cards on the floor. Teammate #1 tosses the beanbag at the cards. He or she picks up the card that the beanbag landed on, says the word, and uses a transparency pen to write the word on the correct word family card. The word card goes in a discard pile. The other teammates take turns tossing the beanbag and writing the words on the word family cards.

Word Family Lists

Structure: Jot Thoughts

Teammates cover the table with words, belonging to a word family, written on slips of paper. Each student writes one word per slip of paper and announces the word before placing it in the middle of the table. Each added word needs to be new. (Variation: words, that begin or end the same; words, that were made plural by adding *es*, words ending with -ing, etc.)

Team Word Study Activities
(continued)

Colorful Team Spelling

Structure: RoundTable

Each team member has a different colored pencil or marker. The teacher gives a word. The team passes a paper around the table. Each student adds one letter to spell the word and passes the paper on to the next student until the word is spelled.

Do You Know My Word?

Structure: Showdown

One teammate spells aloud a word. Once the word is spelled, teammates pick up a marker and spell the word on individual dry-erase boards. When the Showdown Captain calls, "Showdown," teammates hold up their boards and show their spellings and name the word. They then celebrate or coach.

Sentence Writing

Structure: RoundTable

Each student on the team has a different colored pencil. Each person adds a word to a paper, which is passed around the table. The words need to form a complete sentence. When the sentence is completed, the sentence is read to the other teams. Each word study word for the week that is used correctly in the sentence is worth one point for class goal.

Find the Errors

Structure: Simultaneous RoundTable

Each team has four teacher-made sentence strips with spelling errors (one for each student). Each student has a different colored pencil. The papers are passed around the table, with each student correcting one error before passing the paper to the next student. Keep passing the sentences around until all the errors have been corrected.

Guess the Letters

Structure: Talking Chips

Use a large dry-erase board or chalkboard, that all team members can see. Teammate #1 looks at a list of words and chooses one word. He or she makes a line for each letter of the word (_ _ _ _). The other team members take turns putting a talking chip in the middle of the table and guessing a letter or the word. If the word is not guessed and all the talking chips have been used, teammates pick up their talking chips and begin guessing again. When the word has been identified, Teammate #2 chooses a new word. Continue until all teammates have had an opportunity to choose a word.

Word Family Web

Structure: RoundTable

Each team works together to create a word family web. A large piece of paper is placed in the center of the team with a word family written in the middle (for example: ick, ate, ip). Each student has a different colored marker. Teammates take turns adding a word to the word family web. The team needs to agree on the spelling of the word before the next person writes.

Team Word Study Activities

(continued)

Body Spelling

Structure: Team Formations

Each team receives a word on a card. Their task is to use their bodies to spell the word. Each person on the team must be part of the spelling. Other teams guess what word was spelled.

Movement Spelling

Structure: Team Formations

The teacher calls out a word. Each team decides on a repetitive movement to use with each letter. For example, one team may decide to hop on one foot for each letter of the word as they spell it. Teams spell the word for the other teams, after practicing their words and movements at least three times. (Variation: Teams may use a different movement for each letter of the word.)

Spelling Cheerleaders

Structure: Team Formations

Students in teams act out the given word with their bodies, showing the tall letters (stretching tall with hands over heads), short letters (putting arms straight out or on hips), and tail letters (squatting or touching toes). For example, "Give me a ____. Give me an ____. Give me a __."

Machine Spelling

Structure: Team Line-Ups

Each student on a team becomes one letter of the word being spelled. They line up in order. The word is spelled orally with each student saying his or her word while making a body motion. The team becomes a "word machine." Teams demonstrate their machines to the other teams.

Word Line-Ups

Structure: Team Line-Ups

Each team receives a stack of scrambled letters, which spell a word. Each teammate takes one of the letters. (Teammates may need to take more than one letter or share a letter, depending on the length of the word.) Each team tries to be the first to line up holding the letters in the correct order to spell the word. (If a team member has two letters, which are not positioned side by side in the word, the team will need to be creative in solving the problem.) Teams share their words with other teams.

Word Practice

Structure: Team-Pair-Solo

Teams work together to spell a word. Then teams divide into pairs and spell the same word. They compare with the other pair. Finally, individuals spell the word. They come back together as a team and compare. They celebrate or coach and begin the process with a new word.

Team Word Study Activities
(continued)

Spelling Word Collage

Structure: Team Word-Webbing

Roll out a large piece of paper on the floor or tape one to a wall for each team. Each student has a different colored marker. In a set amount of time, each student tries to fit in as many word study words as possible on the paper to create a colorful word collage.

Pick a Letter, Any Letter

Structure: Think-Write-RoundRobin

Each team has a bag of letters. Teammate #1 chooses a letter from the bag without looking and announces the letter to the team, placing it in the middle. Each student thinks about possible words beginning with that letter and then makes a list of words beginning with that letter on individual dry-erase boards. Time is called after a preset time limit. Teammates take turns RoundRobin sharing one of the words on their lists. If a shared word is also on their lists, students may put a mark by it. Words shared aloud must be new words not previously shared. Continue sharing until all new words have been shared. If a teammate does not have a new word on the list to share, he or she may try to come up with another word.

Spelling Walk

Structure: Traveling Heads Together

Teams huddle to make sure all can spell a given word correctly. Use dry-erase boards to practice writing the word. When everyone is confident they can spell the word, the dry-erase boards are cleared and the team sits down. The teacher calls a number and the student with that number travels to a new team with his or her cleared dry-erase board and a marker. At the new team, the student shares the spelling of the word by writing it on the dry-erase board.

Spelling Toss

Structure: Turn Toss

Teammates toss a ball to each other. As each teammate catches the ball, he or she contributes a letter to the spelling of a word called out by the teacher. Teammates continue until the word is spelled. The teacher then gives a new word.

Class Word Study Activities

Add a Word to My Family

Structure: Find Someone Who

Students have bingo sheets. At the top they put a word given by the teacher. They circulate throughout the room looking for someone who can add a word to a square on their paper and sign his or her name below the added word. The word needs to belong to the same family as the given word and needs to be one that is not already on the paper.

Spell My Word

Structure: Inside-Outside Circle

Students form two circles facing each other. Each student has a word list. As either the outside or the inside circle moves one space, students face new partners. Partners take turns having their partner spell a word from the list. Rotate.

What's My Word?

Structure: Who Am I?

Students attempt to determine their secret word (taped on their back) by circulating and asking "yes/no" questions of classmates. They are allowed three questions per classmate (or unlimited questions until they receive a "no" response). They then find a new classmate to question. When the student guesses his or her word, the student becomes a consultant to give clues to those who have not yet found their identity.

Jumping Words

Structure: Take Off, Touch Down

Give each student a word card. The teacher calls out a vowel sound. If the student's word contains the vowel sound, he or she stands or jumps up. Standing students share their words simultaneously. Teacher and class check for accuracy. The teacher continues to call vowel sounds as students listen for the vowel sound in their words. Variation: The teacher calls out a word and students jump up when they hear a word, that rhymes with the word on their word card.

How Many?

Structure: Mix-Freeze-Group

Students make groups with a specific number of students corresponding to answers to questions, asked by the teacher, such as:
- # of total letters in a given word
- # of vowels in a word
- # of a specific letter in a word
- # of syllables in a word

(For example, if the answer to the question is four, when the teacher calls, "Show me," students show the number 4 with their fingers on their chests, quickly form groups of four, and kneel down. Students not finding a group should meet in a predetermined part of the room in "Lost and Found.")

Making Words Lesson Plans

On the following pages are three lessons designed to help students think about the sounds they hear in words and the letter patterns that make up those sounds. They all involve making words from one longer word. The steps for the three lessons are the same. In each of the three lessons, students proceed through three activities:

- **Activity 1: Making Words** (RallyCoach)
- **Activity 2: Sorting** (Find My Rule)
- **Activity 3: Transfer** (RallyCoach)

Since the steps are the same for all three lesson, we will provide a full description of Lesson 1, then just provide the necessary substitutions for Lessons 2 and 3.

Each lesson has its own set of blacklines, but they all share the Find My Rule Mat on page 220. Also, you will find two forms to plan and create your own Making Words lessons.

- **Making Words Planning Form** (p. 221)
- **Making Words Student Form** (p. 222)

The Magic Word

When done with each lesson, challenge pairs to see if they can discover the "Magic Word." The magic word is the word made from all the letters from each set of student letters.

The magic words from each lesson are:
Lesson 1: weather
Lesson 2: cereals
Lesson 3: permanent

Helpful Hints:

- These activities may be done in one day or two days at the beginning of the week. Making Words may be done on day one and the Sorting and Transfer activities on day two.
- Mailing envelopes or plastic sandwich baggies will help students keep their materials organized and accessible.
- These activities are most beneficial when the teacher selects or designs lessons that reinforce letter patterns the students are needing to know or strengthen for their reading and writing.
- All letters on the Making Words form are put in alphabetical order with vowels first, followed by consonants.

Making Words Lessons

Lessons

Making Words
Lesson 1: "Weather"

Activity 1: Making Words

In pairs, students take turns manipulating letter cards to make words.

STRUCTURE
RallyCoach

Activity 1 Steps

1. The teacher makes a transparency of the Making Words (Weather) page and cuts out the letters and words.

2. Each pair receives one set of the following letters: *a, e, e, h, r, t, w* (the letters from the word *weather*) from the blackline.

3. The teacher asks students to make words as described in the table on page 207, Words to Make from *Weather*. The teacher reviews the teaching points as indicated on the table.

4. Partner A makes the first word, while Partner B coaches if necessary.

5. The teacher makes the word on the overhead projector.

6. Students write the word in a box on their student form. They will use these words in Activity 2.

7. Partners take turns for each new word and the process is repeated.

Blacklines

Words to Make from *Weather*

Directions	Word	Teaching Point
Make: *tree*	tree	
Add a letter to make a new word	three	Discuss /ee/ and /th/ sounds/pattern
Make: *eat*	eat	
Add an ending to *eat*.	eater	Discuss decoding words with endings.
Add a beginning letter to make a new word.	heater	Discuss using familiar letter patterns to decode words.
Take off the /er/ ending. Add a letter to make a new word.	wheat	
Make: *ear*	ear	Discuss /ee/, /ea/ making the same sound.
Add a letter to make a new word. I can hear the birds singing.	hear	
Make a homophone for *hear*. Please come here to my table.	here	Homophones = same sound/different spelling
Add a letter to make a new word.	there	Discuss tricky part of word.
Change one letter to make a new word. Where are my shoes?	where	Discuss familiar letter pattern in *there* and *where*.
Make a homophone for *where*. I will wear my jacket today.	wear	Discuss the sound for /ea/ and the importance of trying words with long sound/short sound of /ea/.
Change the beginning letter to make a new word. There is a tear in my jeans. I saw a tear in your eyes.	tear	Try vowel pattern with both the long and short sound of /ea/. Note that it will make a word both ways. Students will need to use context to figure out the correct word meaning.
Use all the letters to make the magic word.	weather	Discuss letter patterns.

Activity 2: Sorting

The teacher places words in two different columns on the overhead projector. The challenge is for students to discover the teacher's rules for sorting the words this way. This activity draws the students' attention to visual clues and letter patterns.

STRUCTURE

Find My Rule

Ideas for Rules

- **homophones**
- **long /ea/ words**
- **short /ea/ words**
- **two consonants that make one sound: th, wh**
- **letter pattern /ear/**
- **letter pattern /eat/**

Activity 2 Steps

1. The teacher makes a transparency of the Find My Rule Mat (page 220).

2. The teacher decides on a "rule" to place words in the two different columns of the Mat. For the example below, the rule is **long /ea/ words.**

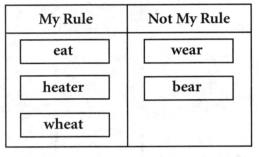

My Rule	Not My Rule
eat	wear
heater	bear
wheat	

3. The teacher places one word in each column, and asks, "What is my rule?"

4. Students RallyRobin with their shoulder partners to determine what the rule may be.

5. The teacher adds the next two words, one in each column, and asks again, "What is my rule?"

6. Students RallyRobin again.

7. This continues until students think they know the rule. The teacher calls on students to verbalize the rule. If correct, the teacher congratulates the students, if incorrect the process continues.

8. When done, the activity may be repeated with a new rule. Other rule examples are listed at left.

9. After practice, students can cut apart their word boxes from Activity 1, step 6. They can create their own word sorts and have a partner find the rule.

Blacklines

Activity 3: Transfer

The teacher displays a word card on the overhead projector and discusses the letter pattern. Then the teacher says, "If you can spell this word, you can also spell..." Students work in pairs to spell the new word. This activity helps students "use what they know" from one word and transfer it to a new word that they are trying to read or write.

STRUCTURE
RallyCoach

Activity 3 Steps

1. The teacher places a word card on the overhead projector.

2. The teacher states, "If you can spell this word, you can also spell…." (See the examples below.)

3. Partner A spells the word while Partner B watches, checks, and coaches as needed.

4. The teacher spells the new word for the class, and students praise their partners for correct spelling.

5. Students switch roles of Speller and Coach for each new word.

Using What You Know

If you can spell…	Then you can spell…
heat	neat, beat, meat
weather	feather
tree	free, spree, glee
hear	fear, smear, dear

Making Words (Weather)
Teacher Transparency Form

Instructions: Make a transparency of this page. Cut out letters and words to use during Activity 1: Making Words and with Activity 2: Sorting.

	heater	there			
	eater	here	weather		
w	eat	hear	tear		
r					
t					
h	three	ear	wear		
e					
e					
a	tree	wheat	where		

Making Words (a, e, e, h, r, t, w)
Student Form

Instructions: Make one copy per student. Cut apart letters to use during Activity 1: Making Words. Cut apart boxes after words are added during Activity 2: Sorting.

Lesson 2: "Cereals"
Activity 1: Making Words

The steps for this activity are the same as Lesson 1, Activity 1 but substitute the following words to make from the letters in Cereals.

Words to Make from *Cereals*

Directions	Word	Teaching Point
Make: *see* I see a beautiful rainbow.	see	
Change one letter to make another word.	sea	Homophones = same sound/different spelling Discuss /ee/ and /ea/ making the same sound.
Make: *are* Are you my friend?	are	
Rearrange the letters to make a new word.	ear	
Make *ear* plural.	ears	
Remove the *s* and add a blend to the beginning.	clear	Decoding: cover up from the vowel through the rest of the word, say the blend, then uncover and say the whole word.
Remove the *c.* Take the beginning letter and end letter and switch them.	real	
Make a homophone for *real.* The fishing reel was a gift.	reel	Homophones Review /ee/ and /ea/ sounds.
Make: *car* The car was zooming down my street.	car	
Add a silent *e.*	care	
Add a beginning letter to make a new word.	scare	Practice decoding with a blend.
Take away the silent *e.*	scar	
Make: *scale*	scale	
Take away one letter.	sale	
Add a prefix: *re.*	resale	Discuss meaning of prefix /re/ ("again").
Make: *ace* The ace is missing from the card deck.	ace	Why does the *c* make an *s* sound? (Rule: when *i*, *e*, or *y* follows a *c*, the *c* will make /s/).
Add a beginning letter.	race	Decoding: use letter pattern.

Balanced Literacy • Third Grade • Skidmore & Graber
Kagan Publishing • 1 (800) 933-2667 • www.KaganOnline.com

Directions	Word	Teaching Point
Make: *cease*	cease	/c/ = /s/ sound.
Add a letter to make a new word.	crease	/c/ = /k/ sound.
Remove the blend and add a letter.	lease	
Remove the *l* and put it at the end.	easel	Use what you know to decode.
Use all the letters to make the magic word.	cereals	Review /c/ = /s/ and /ea/ sounds.

Activity 2: Sorting

The steps for this activity are the same as Lesson 1, Activity 2. Below is an example for Find My Rule using the Cereals words and additional ideas for Find My Rule.

Ideas for Rules

• **long /ea/**
• **homophones**
• **blends**
• **hard and soft /c/ sounds**

My Rule	Not My Rule
cease	crease
cereal	

Example: soft sound of *c*

Activity 3: Transfer

The steps for this activity are the same as Lesson 1, Activity 3, except use the following words to spell.

Using What You Know
If you can spell…	Then you can spell…
crease	grease, please
ace	place, trace, space

Making Words (Cereals)
Teacher Transparency Form

Instructions: Make a transparency of this page. Cut out letters and words to use during Activity 1: Making Words.

a e e c l r s	ears	care	resale	lease		
	ear	car	sale	crease		
	are	reel	scale	cease		
	sea	real	scar	race	cereals	
	see	clear	scare	ace	easel	

Making Words (a, e, e, c, l, r, s)
Student Form

Instructions: Make one copy per student. Cut apart letters to use during Activity 1: Making Words. Cut apart boxes after words are added during Acitvity 2: Sorting.

s r l c e a

Lesson 3: "Permanent"
Activity 1: Making Words

The steps for this activity are the same as Lesson 1, Activity 1 but substitute the following words to make from the letters in Permanent.

Words to Make from *Permanent*

Directions	Word	Teaching Point
Make: *rat*	rat	
Add a silent *e* at the end of the word. What is the new word?	rate	Discuss how silent *e* changes the vowel sound. Use the word in a sentence to clarify meaning.
Make: *pan*	pan	
Add a silent *e* at the end of the word. What is the new word?	pane	Use the word in a sentence to clarify meaning. Discuss the homophones *pain/pane*.
Make: *mane*	mane	Use the word in a sentence to clarify meaning. Discuss the homophones *main/mane*.
Remove the silent *e*. What is the new word?	man	
Place the *e* back in the word to spell *mean*.	mean	Discuss the long sound of /ea/.
Make: *pear*	pear	Discuss the sound of /ea/.
Remove the *p* and what is the word?	ear	Discuss how the /ea/ letter pattern changed.
Make: *are*	are	
Replace the *e* with another letter to make the word *art*.	art	Discuss the /ar/ letter pattern.
Add a letter to spell *part*.	part	
Rearrange the letters to spell a new word.	trap	
Make: *rent*	rent	Discuss the /en/ letter pattern
Make: *men*	men	
Make: *ten*	ten	
Rearrange the letters to spell a new word.	net	
Make: *tea*	tea	What letter pattern helped you spell this word?
Rearrange the letters to spell a new word.	eat	

Balanced Literacy • Third Grade • Skidmore & Graber
Kagan Publishing • 1 (800) 933-2667 • www.KaganOnline.com

Words to Make from "Permanent" (continued)

Directions	Word	Teaching Point
Add a letter to spell *neat*.	neat	
Replace the *n* with an *m*.	meat	
Rearrange the letters to spell a new word.	team	
Use all the letters to make a magic word.	permanent	Use the word in a sentence to clarify meaning.

Activity 2: Sorting

The steps for this activity are the same as Lesson 1, Activity 2. Below is an example for Find My Rule using the Permanent words and additional ideas for Find My Rule.

Ideas for Rules

- silent *e*
- long /ea/
- short /ea/
- letter pattern /ar/
- letter pattern /en/

My Rule	Not My Rule
mean	fear
meat	bear
team	

Example: long /ea/ words

Activity 3: Transfer

The steps for this activity are the same as Lesson 1, Activity 3, except use the following words to spell.

Using What You Know

If you can spell…	Then you can spell…
rent	spent, sent, bent
rate	state, skate, late
team	steam, dream, cream

Making Words (Permanent)
Teacher Transparency Form

Instructions: Make a transparency of this page. Cut out letters and words to use during Activity 1: Making Words.

t	mane	are	men	neat
r	pane	ear	rent	eat
p	pan	pear	trap	tea
n	rate	mean	part	net
e	rat	man	art	ten
a				meat

permanent

team

Balanced Literacy • Third Grade • Skidmore & Graber
Kagan Publishing • 1 (800) 933-2667 • www.KaganOnline.com

Making Words (a, e, e, n, n, m p, r, t)
Student Form

Instructions: Make one copy per student. Cut apart letters to use during Activity 1: Making Words.
Cut apart boxes after words are added during Activity 2: Sorting.

t

r

p

n

m

e

a

Find My Rule Mat
for Making Words

Instructions: Make a transparency of this mat for Activity 2: Sorting. Make copies for each pair of students for Activity 2: Sorting.

My Rule	Not My Rule

Making Words Planning Form

Letters: _____

Magic Word: _____

Part 1: Making Words (RallyTable)

Instructions: Use this planning form to create additional Making Words lessons.

Directions	Word	Teaching Point

Part 2: Sorting (Find My Rule)	Sort For:

Part 3: Transfer (RallyCoach)	Using What You Know

Making Words
Student Form

Instructions: Use this planning form to create the letters and words for additional Making Words lessons.

Who Knows?

Students mix about the room, finding others who can help them fill out their Find Someone Who word study worksheets.

STRUCTURE

Find Someone Who

Activity Steps

1. Every student receives a Find Someone Who worksheet.

2. Students mix around the room until they find a partner.

3. In pairs, Partner A asks a question from the worksheet; Partner B responds. Partner A records the answer on his or her worksheet.

4. Partner B checks and initials the answer.

5. Partner B asks a question. Partner A responds. Partner B records the answer on his or her worksheet.

6. Partner A checks and initials the answer.

7. Partners shake hands, part, and raise a hand again as they search for a new partner.

8. Students repeat the process until they complete their worksheets.

9. When their worksheets are completed, students sit down; seated students may be approached by others as a resource.

10. In teams, students compare answers; if there is disagreement or uncertainty, they raise four hands to ask a team question.

Blacklines

All About Contractions!

Find Someone Who

Name _____

Instructions: Copy one page per student.

All About Contractions!

Choose the correct contraction and write the word in the blank.

• I _____ eaten the whole thing!

• Mom _____ made supper yet.

• _____ go to the park.

> let's
>
> could've
>
> hasn't

Initials

All About Contractions!

Draw lines to connect the partners.

here's	we are
we're	I have
I've	must not
mustn't	here is

Initials

All About Contractions!

Add apostrophes (') to make contractions:

couldve

shes

arent

Initials

All About Contractions!

Draw lines to connect the partners.

I'd	I am
I'll	I have
I've	I will
I'm	I would

Initials

All About Contractions!

Is or Has?

Write the correct two words in the blank. Reread the sentence to make sure it makes sense.

(She's) _____ my best friend.
    (She is or She has)

(She's) _____ been here before.
    (She is or She has)

Initials

All About Contractions!

Circle the contractions.

sailboat

that's

its

aren't

students'

isn't

his

Initials

All About Contractions!

Circle the contraction in each sentence.

• Let's go to the park to play baseball.

• I was so excited that I couldn't sleep last night!

Initials

All About ur, ir, er

Find Someone Who

Name _____

Instructions: Copy one page per student.

All About ur, ir, er

Which way looks right?
Circle it.

bird

burd

berd

Initials

All About ur, ir, er

Add
ir, er, ur

ch _ _ ch

sh _ _ t

s _ _ ve

Initials

All About ur, ir, er

Circle the misspelled word in each sentence.

• **The boy's shert is blue.**

• **Tirn right at the flashing light.**

• **She is furst in line.**

Initials

All About ur, ir, er

Make a rhyme:

churn

turn

__ urn

Initials

All About ur, ir, er

These words are all missing the same two letters. Fill in the letters.
(er, ir, ur)

moth _ _

lett _ _

ov _ _

Initials

All About ur, ir, er

Choose three of the following words and use them in a complete sentence.

girl   twirl   skirt   nurse

burn   stern

_____

_____

_____

_____

Initials

All About Compound Words!

Find Someone Who

Name _____

Instructions: Copy one page per student.

All About Compound Words!

Match

fire	father
eye	lash
heart	cracker
flag	burn
step	pole

Initials

All About Compound Words!

Draw a line to divide each compound word into two complete words.

horseback

motorcycle

heavyweight

rollerblade

Initials

All About Compound Words!

Underline the compound word in each sentence.

- Snowballs were flying all around me as I walked across the yard.
- The winding staircase led to a dark attic in my cousin's house.
- I want to visit the country of England someday.

Initials

All About Compound Words!

Can you write a compound word not on this page? (Look in a book or around the room.)

_____

Initials

All About Compound Words!

Write the definition of a compound word.

_____

_____

_____

_____

Initials

All About Compound Words!

Circle the compound words.

what's

whatever

doesn't

something

Initials

All About Compound Words!

Circle the compound words that you can correctly read to your partner.

wasteland

weatherman

sleepwalking

sightseeing

Initials

Skill Review

Find Someone Who

Name _____

Instructions: Copy one page per student.

Skill Review

Circle the two homophones in the sentence.

On cold winter days, my grandfather would chop wood for the fire.

Initials

Skill Review

Write the plural form for each word.

foot _____

mouse _____

woman _____

Initials

Skill Review

Which words look right? Circle them.

chirp
churp

screem
scream

fruit
froot

Initials

Skill Review

Write the two words that make up the contraction in each sentence.

• I'd rather drink water than soda. _____ _____

• I could've been here sooner, but my mom needed me to run an errand. _____ _____

Initials

Skill Review

Write the correct vowel pattern for each word.

(ir, igh, ow, ea)

m ___ t

tw ___ l

t ___ ch

sc ___ l

Initials

Skill Review

Circle the short /ea/ words.

weather

wheat

leap

cream

feather

heavy

Initials

Skill Review

Circle the word that is not used correctly in each sentence.

• When I went on vacation, I got to sea a dolphin jump.

• You our my best friend.

Initials

Find Someone Who Form

Name _____

Instructions: Use this form to create questions for additional activities.

| | Initials |

| | Initials |
| | Initials |

| | Initials |

	Initials
	Initials
	Initials

Partner Word Study Practice

To practice antonyms, synonyms, contractions, prefixes, and letter patterns, students quiz a partner, get quizzed by a partner, and then trade cards to repeat the process with a new partner.

Activity Steps

STRUCTURE

Quiz-Quiz-Trade

1 Each student receives a card with a question on the front and answer on the back.

2 All students stand up, put a hand up, and pair up.

3 Partner A quizzes Partner B.

4 Partner B answers.

5 Partner A checks the answer on back and praises or coaches.

6 Partners switch roles and quiz again.

7 After they have quizzed both ways, partners trade cards, and raise their hands to find a new partner. The partner quizzing and trading proceeds for numerous pairings.

Front

Question:

Say the word. Which way looks right?

a) boil
b) boyl

Back

Answer:

a) boil

Blacklines

Antonyms: Words That Mean the Opposite
Quiz-Quiz-Trade

Instructions: Copy enough cards so each student has one card. Cut on dotted lines and fold in half.

Antonyms: Words That Mean the Opposite	Antonyms: Words That Mean the Opposite
Question What is an antonym for shallow? a) deep b) thin	**Answer** What is an antonym for shallow? ## a) deep
Question What is an antonym for innocent? a) harmless b) guilty	**Answer** What is an antonym for innocent? ## b) guilty
Question What is an antonym for destroy? a) create b) ruin	**Answer** What is an antonym for destroy? ## a) create
Question What is an antonym for unknown? a) familiar b) strange	**Answer** What is an antonym for unknown? ## a) familiar

Antonyms: Words That Mean the Opposite

Quiz-Quiz-Trade

Instructions: Copy enough cards so each student has one card. Cut on dotted lines and fold in half.

Antonyms: Words That Mean the Opposite

Question

What is an antonym for simple?

    a) easy
    b) difficult

Antonyms: Words That Mean the Opposite

Answer

What is an antonym for simple?

b) difficult

Antonyms: Words That Mean the Opposite

Question

What is an antonym for always?

    a) never
    b) often

Antonyms: Words That Mean the Opposite

Answer

What is an antonym for always?

a) never

Antonyms: Words That Mean the Opposite

Question

What is an antonym for laugh?

    a) sob
    b) silly

Antonyms: Words That Mean the Opposite

Answer

What is an antonym for laugh?

a) sob

Antonyms: Words That Mean the Opposite

Question

What is an antonym for noisy?

    a) loud
    b) quiet

Antonyms: Words That Mean the Opposite

Answer

What is an antonym for noisy?

b) quiet

Antonyms: Words That Mean the Opposite
Quiz-Quiz-Trade

Instructions: Copy enough cards so each student has one card. Cut on dotted lines and fold in half.

Antonyms: Words That Mean the Opposite

Question

What is an antonym for remember?

    a) memorize
    b) forget

Antonyms: Words That Mean the Opposite

Answer

What is an antonym for remember?

b) forget

Antonyms: Words That Mean the Opposite

Question

What is an antonym for dangerous?

    a) harmless
    b) harmful

Antonyms: Words That Mean the Opposite

Answer

What is an antonym for dangerous?

a) harmless

Antonyms: Words That Mean the Opposite

Question

What is an antonym for healthy?

    a) sick
    b) strong

Antonyms: Words That Mean the Opposite

Answer

What is an antonym for healthy?

a) sick

Antonyms: Words That Mean the Opposite

Question

What is an antonym for empty?

    a) full
    b) blank

Antonyms: Words That Mean the Opposite

Answer

What is an antonym for empty?

a) full

Antonyms: Words That Mean the Opposite
Quiz-Quiz-Trade

Instructions: Copy enough cards so each student has one card. Cut on dotted lines and fold in half.

Antonyms: Words That Mean the Opposite	Antonyms: Words That Mean the Opposite

Question
 	
What is an antonym for tight?
 	
   a) firm
   b) loose
	Answer
	
	What is an antonym for tight?
	
	## b) loose

Question
 	
What is an antonym for friend?
 	
   a) buddy
   b) enemy
	Answer
	
	What is an antonym for friend?
	
	## b) enemy

Question
 	
What is an antonym for straight?
 	
   a) bent
   b) not curved
	Answer
	
	What is an antonym for straight?
	
	## a) bent

Question
 	
What is an antonym for city?
 	
   a) country
   b) town
	Answer
	
	What is an antonym for city?
	
	## a) country

Antonyms: Words That Mean the Opposite

Mean the Opposite

Quiz-Quiz-Trade

Instructions: Copy enough cards so each student has one card. Cut on dotted lines and fold in half.

Antonyms: Words That Mean the Opposite	Antonyms: Words That Mean the Opposite
Question What is an antonym for lead? a) follow b) guide	**Answer** What is an antonym for lead? ## a) follow
Question What is an antonym for reward? a) acknowledge b) punish	**Answer** What is an antonym for reward? ## b) punish
Question What is an antonym for early? a) late b) prompt	**Answer** What is an antonym for early? ## a) late
Question What is an antonym for narrow? a) wide b) slim	**Answer** What is an antonym for narrow? ## a) wide

Balanced Literacy • Third Grade • Skidmore & Graber
Kagan Publishing • 1 (800) 933-2667 • www.KaganOnline.com

Antonyms: Words That Mean the Opposite
Quiz-Quiz-Trade

Instructions: Copy enough cards so each student has one card. Cut on dotted lines and fold in half.

Antonyms: Words That Mean the Opposite

Question

What is an antonym for busy?

    a) idle
    b) hurried

Antonyms: Words That Mean the Opposite

Answer

What is an antonym for busy?

a) idle

Antonyms: Words That Mean the Opposite

Question

What is an antonym for dangerous?

    a) hurtful
    b) safe

Antonyms: Words That Mean the Opposite

Answer

What is an antonym for dangerous?

b) safe

Antonyms: Words That Mean the Opposite

Question

What is an antonym for capture?

    a) catch
    b) release

Antonyms: Words That Mean the Opposite

Answer

What is an antonym for capture?

b) release

Antonyms: Words That Mean the Opposite

Question

What is an antonym for expensive?

    a) cheap
    b) costly

Antonyms: Words That Mean the Opposite

Answer

What is an antonym for expensive?

a) cheap

Antonyms: Words That Mean the Opposite

Quiz-Quiz-Trade

Instructions: Copy enough cards so each student has one card. Cut on dotted lines and fold in half.

Antonyms: Words That Mean the Opposite

Question

What is an antonym for failure?

    a) success
    b) omit

Antonyms: Words That Mean the Opposite

Answer

What is an antonym for failure?

a) success

Antonyms: Words That Mean the Opposite

Question

What is an antonym for miss?

    a) lose
    b) hit

Antonyms: Words That Mean the Opposite

Answer

What is an antonym for miss?

b) hit

Antonyms: Words That Mean the Opposite

Question

What is an antonym for freeze?

    a) melt
    b) chill

Antonyms: Words That Mean the Opposite

Answer

What is an antonym for freeze?

a) melt

Antonyms: Words That Mean the Opposite

Question

What is an antonym for tame?

    a) pet
    b) wild

Antonyms: Words That Mean the Opposite

Answer

What is an antonym for tame?

b) wild

Synonyms: Words That Have the Same or Almost the Same Meaning

Quiz-Quiz-Trade

Instructions: Copy enough cards so each student has one card. Cut on dotted lines and fold in half.

Synonyms: Words That Have the Same or Almost the Same Meaning

Question

What is an synonym for rocks?

  a) beach
  b) stones

Synonyms: Words That Have the Same or Almost the Same Meaning

Answer

What is an synonym for rocks?

b) stones

Synonyms: Words That Have the Same or Almost the Same Meaning

Question

What is an synonym for giant?

  a) tiny
  b) huge

Synonyms: Words That Have the Same or Almost the Same Meaning

Answer

What is an synonym for giant?

b) huge

Synonyms: Words That Have the Same or Almost the Same Meaning

Question

What is an synonym for sleigh?

  a) sled
  b) carriage

Synonyms: Words That Have the Same or Almost the Same Meaning

Answer

What is an synonym for sleigh?

a) sled

Synonyms: Words That Have the Same or Almost the Same Meaning

Question

What is an synonym for flame?

  a) match
  b) fire

Synonyms: Words That Have the Same or Almost the Same Meaning

Answer

What is an synonym for flame?

b) fire

Synonyms: Words That Have the Same or Almost the Same Meaning
Quiz-Quiz-Trade

Instructions: Copy enough cards so each student has one card. Cut on dotted lines and fold in half.

Synonyms: Words That Have the Same or Almost the Same Meaning	Synonyms: Words That Have the Same or Almost the Same Meaning

Question
 	
What is an synonym for pieces?
 	
   a) parts
   b) whole
	Answer
	
	What is an synonym for pieces?
	
	## a) parts

Question
 	
What is an synonym for laugh?
 	
   a) sorrow
   b) giggle
	Answer
	
	What is an synonym for laugh?
	
	## b) giggle

Question
 	
What is an synonym for friend?
 	
   a) stranger
   b) pal
	Answer
	
	What is an synonym for friend?
	
	## b) pal

Question
 	
What is an synonym for sick?
 	
   a) ill
   b) healthy
	Answer
	
	What is an synonym for sick?
	
	## a) ill

Synonyms: Words That Have the Same or Almost the Same Meaning
Quiz-Quiz-Trade

Instructions: Copy enough cards so each student has one card. Cut on dotted lines and fold in half.

Synonyms: Words That Have the Same or Almost the Same Meaning

Question

What is an synonym for pail?

   a) spoon
   b) bucket

Synonyms: Words That Have the Same or Almost the Same Meaning

Answer

What is an synonym for pail?

b) bucket

Synonyms: Words That Have the Same or Almost the Same Meaning

Question

What is an synonym for exit?

   a) depart
   b) enter

Synonyms: Words That Have the Same or Almost the Same Meaning

Answer

What is an synonym for exit?

a) depart

Synonyms: Words That Have the Same or Almost the Same Meaning

Question

What is an synonym for destroy?

   a) ruin
   b) rebuild

Synonyms: Words That Have the Same or Almost the Same Meaning

Answer

What is an synonym for destroy?

a) ruin

Synonyms: Words That Have the Same or Almost the Same Meaning

Question

What is an synonym for gaze?

   a) stare
   b) blink

Synonyms: Words That Have the Same or Almost the Same Meaning

Answer

What is an synonym for gaze?

a) stare

Synonyms: Words That Have the Same or Almost the Same Meaning
Quiz-Quiz-Trade

Instructions: Copy enough cards so each student has one card. Cut on dotted lines and fold in half.

Synonyms: Words That Have the Same or Almost the Same Meaning

Question

What is an synonym for hide?

    a) unveil
    b) disguise

Synonyms: Words That Have the Same or Almost the Same Meaning

Answer

What is an synonym for hide?

b) disguise

Synonyms: Words That Have the Same or Almost the Same Meaning

Question

What is an synonym for repair?

    a) fix
    b) break

Synonyms: Words That Have the Same or Almost the Same Meaning

Answer

What is an synonym for repair?

a) fix

Synonyms: Words That Have the Same or Almost the Same Meaning

Question

What is an synonym for answer?

    a) question
    b) solution

Synonyms: Words That Have the Same or Almost the Same Meaning

Answer

What is an synonym for answer?

b) solution

Synonyms: Words That Have the Same or Almost the Same Meaning

Question

What is an synonym for sleep?

    a) awake
    b) snooze

Synonyms: Words That Have the Same or Almost the Same Meaning

Answer

What is an synonym for sleep?

b) snooze

Synonyms: Words That Have the Same or Almost the Same Meaning
Quiz-Quiz-Trade

Instructions: Copy enough cards so each student has one card. Cut on dotted lines and fold in half.

Synonyms: Words That Have the Same or Almost the Same Meaning

Question

What is an synonym for smart?

    a) ignorant
    b) intelligent

Synonyms: Words That Have the Same or Almost the Same Meaning

Answer

What is an synonym for smart?

b) intelligent

Synonyms: Words That Have the Same or Almost the Same Meaning

Question

What is an synonym for witnessed?

    a) observed
    b) unaware

Synonyms: Words That Have the Same or Almost the Same Meaning

Answer

What is an synonym for witnessed?

a) observed

Synonyms: Words That Have the Same or Almost the Same Meaning

Question

What is an synonym for triumphant?

    a) victorious
    b) defeat

Synonyms: Words That Have the Same or Almost the Same Meaning

Answer

What is an synonym for triumphant?

a) victorious

Synonyms: Words That Have the Same or Almost the Same Meaning

Question

What is an synonym for certainly?

    a) unsure
    b) definitely

Synonyms: Words That Have the Same or Almost the Same Meaning

Answer

What is an synonym for certainly?

b) definitely

Synonyms: Words That Have the Same or Almost the Same Meaning
Quiz-Quiz-Trade

Instructions: Copy enough cards so each student has one card. Cut on dotted lines and fold in half.

Synonyms: Words That Have the Same or Almost the Same Meaning	Synonyms: Words That Have the Same or Almost the Same Meaning
Question What is an synonym for turn? a) stay b) rotate	**Answer** What is an synonym for turn? ## b) rotate
Question What is an synonym for ground? a) land b) air	**Answer** What is an synonym for ground? ## a) land
Question What is an synonym for study? a) examine b) ignore	**Answer** What is an synonym for study? ## a) examine
Question What is an synonym for example? a) exception b) model	**Answer** What is an synonym for example? ## b) model

Synonyms: Words That Have the Same or Almost the Same Meaning
Quiz-Quiz-Trade

Instructions: Copy enough cards so each student has one card. Cut on dotted lines and fold in half.

Synonyms: Words That Have the Same or Almost the Same Meaning

Question

What is an synonym for remember?

    a) recall
    b) forget

Synonyms: Words That Have the Same or Almost the Same Meaning

Answer

What is an synonym for remember?

a) recall

Synonyms: Words That Have the Same or Almost the Same Meaning

Question

What is an synonym for next?

    a) following
    b) before

Synonyms: Words That Have the Same or Almost the Same Meaning

Answer

What is an synonym for next?

a) following

Synonyms: Words That Have the Same or Almost the Same Meaning

Question

What is an synonym for often?

    a) never
    b) frequently

Synonyms: Words That Have the Same or Almost the Same Meaning

Answer

What is an synonym for often?

b) frequently

Synonyms: Words That Have the Same or Almost the Same Meaning

Question

What is an synonym for generous?

    a) rude
    b) giving

Synonyms: Words That Have the Same or Almost the Same Meaning

Answer

What is an synonym for generous?

b) giving

Contractions
Quiz-Quiz-Trade

Instructions: Copy enough cards so each student has one card. Cut on dotted lines and fold in half.

Contractions	Contractions
Spell the contraction (aloud or on paper). **Question** What contraction can be made with these two words? **could have**	**Answer** **could've**
Spell the contraction (aloud or on paper). **Question** What contraction can be made with these two words? **I have**	**Answer** **I've**
Spell the contraction (aloud or on paper). **Question** What contraction can be made with these two words? **might have**	**Answer** **might've**
Spell the contraction (aloud or on paper). **Question** What contraction can be made with these two words? **should have**	**Answer** **should've**

Balanced Literacy • Third Grade • Skidmore & Graber
Kagan Publishing • 1 (800) 933-2667 • www.KaganOnline.com

Contractions
Quiz-Quiz-Trade

Instructions: Copy enough cards so each student has one card. Cut on dotted lines and fold in half.

Contractions	Contractions
Spell the contraction (aloud or on paper). **Question** What contraction can be made with these two words? **they have**	**Answer** **they've**
Spell the contraction (aloud or on paper). **Question** What contraction can be made with these two words? **we have**	**Answer** **we've**
Spell the contraction (aloud or on paper). **Question** What contraction can be made with these two words? **would have**	**Answer** **would've**
Spell the contraction (aloud or on paper). **Question** What contraction can be made with these two words? **you have**	**Answer** **you've**

Contractions
Quiz-Quiz-Trade

Instructions: Copy enough cards so each student has one card. Cut on dotted lines and fold in half.

Contractions	Contractions
Spell the contraction (aloud or on paper). **Question** What contraction can be made with these two words? **here is**	**Answer** **here's**
Spell the contraction (aloud or on paper). **Question** What contraction can be made with these two words? **he is**	**Answer** **he's**
Spell the contraction (aloud or on paper). **Question** What contraction can be made with these two words? **it is**	**Answer** **it's**
Spell the contraction (aloud or on paper). **Question** What contraction can be made with these two words? **she is**	**Answer** **she's**

Contractions
Quiz-Quiz-Trade

Instructions: Copy enough cards so each student has one card. Cut on dotted lines and fold in half.

Contractions	Contractions
Spell the contraction (aloud or on paper). **Question** What contraction can be made with these two words? **that is**	**Answer** **that's**

Contractions	Contractions
Spell the contraction (aloud or on paper). **Question** What contraction can be made with these two words? **there is**	**Answer** **there's**

Contractions	Contractions
Spell the contraction (aloud or on paper). **Question** What contraction can be made with these two words? **what is**	**Answer** **what's**

Contractions	Contractions
Spell the contraction (aloud or on paper). **Question** What contraction can be made with these two words? **where is**	**Answer** **where's**

Contractions
Quiz-Quiz-Trade

Instructions: Copy enough cards so each student has one card. Cut on dotted lines and fold in half.

Contractions	Contractions
Spell the contraction (aloud or on paper). **Question** What contraction can be made with these two words? **he has**	**Answer** **he's**
Spell the contraction (aloud or on paper). **Question** What contraction can be made with these two words? **it has**	**Answer** **it's**
Spell the contraction (aloud or on paper). **Question** What contraction can be made with these two words? **she has**	**Answer** **she's**
Spell the contraction (aloud or on paper). **Question** What contraction can be made with these two words? **that has**	**Answer** **that's**

Balanced Literacy • Third Grade • Skidmore & Graber
Kagan Publishing • 1 (800) 933-2667 • www.KaganOnline.com

Contractions
Quiz-Quiz-Trade

Instructions: Copy enough cards so each student has one card. Cut on dotted lines and fold in half.

Contractions
Spell the contraction (aloud or on paper).
Question
What contraction can be made with these two words?
there has

Contractions
Answer
there's

Contractions
Spell the contraction (aloud or on paper).
Question
What contraction can be made with these two words?
what has

Contractions
Answer
what's

Contractions
Spell the contraction (aloud or on paper).
Question
What contraction can be made with these two words?
where has

Contractions
Answer
where's

Prefixes (mis- and pre-)
Quiz-Quiz-Trade

Instructions: Copy enough cards so each student has one card. Cut on dotted lines and fold in half.

Prefixes (mis- and pre-)

Question

What does this word mean?

prehistoric

Prefixes (mis- and pre-)

Answer

from the time before recorded history

Prefixes (mis- and pre-)

Question

What does this word mean?

preschool

Prefixes (mis- and pre-)

Answer

nursery school; a school for children before they go to kindergarten

---

Prefixes (mis- and pre-)

Question

What does this word mean?

prepaid

Prefixes (mis- and pre-)

Answer

to pay before services; to give money in advance

Prefixes (mis- and pre-)

Question

What does this word mean?

preview

Prefixes (mis- and pre-)

Answer

to view something in advance; to watch a movie before it comes out

---

Prefixes (mis- and pre-)
Quiz-Quiz-Trade

Instructions: Copy enough cards so each student has one card. Cut on dotted lines and fold in half.

Prefixes (mis- and pre-) **Question** What does this word mean? **prefix**	**Prefixes (mis- and pre-)** **Answer** to add or attach something before or in front of something
Prefixes (mis- and pre-) **Question** What does this word mean? **precook**	**Prefixes (mis- and pre-)** **Answer** to cook in advance; to cook before the final cooking
Prefixes (mis- and pre-) **Question** What does this word mean? **pretest**	**Prefixes (mis- and pre-)** **Answer** a test taken for practice; a test taken to determine previous knowledge
Prefixes (mis- and pre-) **Question** What does this word mean? **prepare**	**Prefixes (mis- and pre-)** **Answer** to get ready in advance or before an event or occasion

Prefixes (mis- and pre-)
Quiz-Quiz-Trade

Instructions: Copy enough cards so each student has one card. Cut on dotted lines and fold in half.

Prefixes (mis- and pre-)	Prefixes (mis- and pre-)
Question What does this word mean? **preheat**	**Answer** to make warm before cooking
Question What does this word mean? **precaution**	**Answer** an action taken in advance to protect from danger
Question What does this word mean? **predate**	**Answer** to mark with an earlier time
Question What does this word mean? **prearrange**	**Answer** to organize in advance; to put in order before needed

Prefixes (mis- and pre-)
Quiz-Quiz-Trade

Instructions: Copy enough cards so each student has one card. Cut on dotted lines and fold in half.

Prefixes (mis- and pre-)	Prefixes (mis- and pre-)
Question What does this word mean? **prejudge**	**Answer** to form an opinion before collecting evidence
Question What does this word mean? **premature**	**Answer** occurring too early
Question What does this word mean? **prelude**	**Answer** a piece of music played before the main composition
Question What does this word mean? **precondition**	**Answer** to train in advance

Prefixes (mis- and pre-)
Quiz-Quiz-Trade

Instructions: Copy enough cards so each student has one card. Cut on dotted lines and fold in half.

Prefixes (mis- and pre-)

Question

What does this word mean?

misunderstand

Prefixes (mis- and pre-)

Answer

to comprehend or perceive incorrectly; to have incorrect knowledge

---

Prefixes (mis- and pre-)

Question

What does this word mean?

mishandle

Prefixes (mis- and pre-)

Answer

to deal with clumsily or roughly; to treat wrongly

Prefixes (mis- and pre-)

Question

What does this word mean?

misplace

Prefixes (mis- and pre-)

Answer

to put in the wrong location

Prefixes (mis- and pre-)

Question

What does this word mean?

mislead

Prefixes (mis- and pre-)

Answer

to direct in the wrong direction; to guide incorrectly

Prefixes (mis- and pre-)
Quiz-Quiz-Trade

Instructions: Copy enough cards so each student has one card. Cut on dotted lines and fold in half.

Prefixes (mis- and pre-)	Prefixes (mis- and pre-)
Question What does this word mean? **mistake**	**Answer** to understand wrongly or to identify incorrectly
Question What does this word mean? **mispell**	**Answer** to use incorrect letters or put them in the wrong order
Question What does this word mean? **mismatch**	**Answer** inaccurate fitting together; putting together objects that don't go together
Question What does this word mean? **misprint**	**Answer** to make an error in copying an image or word

Prefixes (mis- and pre-)
Quiz-Quiz-Trade

Instructions: Copy enough cards so each student has one card. Cut on dotted lines and fold in half.

Prefixes (mis- and pre-)	Prefixes (mis- and pre-)
Question What does this word mean? **miscount**	**Answer** to name or list one by one in order inaccurately
Question What does this word mean? **miscue**	**Answer** a blunder or mistake; a mistaken signal
Question What does this word mean? **misdeed**	**Answer** a wrong action
Question What does this word mean? **misinform**	**Answer** to give wrong information

Balanced Literacy • Third Grade • Skidmore & Graber
Kagan Publishing • 1 (800) 933-2667 • www.KaganOnline.com

Prefixes (mis- and pre-)
Quiz-Quiz-Trade

Instructions: Copy enough cards so each student has one card. Cut on dotted lines and fold in half.

Prefixes (mis- and pre-)	Prefixes (mis- and pre-)
Question What does this word mean? **misname**	**Answer** to call by the incorrect label
Question What does this word mean? **misread**	**Answer** to interpret written words incorrectly
Question What does this word mean? **mishap**	**Answer** an unfortunate accident or wrong event
Question What does this word mean? **misdirect**	**Answer** to guide incorrectly

Prefixes (mis- and pre-)
Quiz-Quiz-Trade

Instructions: Copy enough cards so each student has one card. Cut on dotted lines and fold in half.

Prefixes (mis- and pre-)	Prefixes (mis- and pre-)
Question What does this word mean? **misinterpret**	**Answer** to explain incorrectly
Question What does this word mean? **mispronounce**	**Answer** to say a word incorrectly
Question What does this word mean? **misfortune**	**Answer** bad happenings in one's life
Question What does this word mean? **misbehave**	**Answer** to act inappropriately or wrongly

Letter Patterns: oi, oy
Quiz-Quiz-Trade

Instructions: Copy enough cards so each student has one card. Cut on dotted lines and fold in half.

Letter Patterns: oi, oy	Letter Patterns: oi, oy
Question Say the word. Which way looks right? **a) boil** **b) boyl**	**Answer** **a) boil**
Question Say the word. Which way looks right? **a) joyn** **b) join**	**Answer** **b) join**
Question Say the word. Which way looks right? **a) noise** **b) noyce**	**Answer** **a) noise**
Question Say the word. Which way looks right? **a) poyson** **b) poison**	**Answer** **b) poison**

Letter Patterns: oi, oy
Quiz-Quiz-Trade

Instructions: Copy enough cards so each student has one card. Cut on dotted lines and fold in half.

Letter Patterns: oi, oy	Letter Patterns: oi, oy
Question Say the word. Which way looks right? a) voyce b) voice	**Answer** b) voice
Question Say the word. Which way looks right? a) choice b) choyce	**Answer** a) choice
Question Say the word. Which way looks right? a) joynt b) joint	**Answer** b) joint
Question Say the word. Which way looks right? a) rejoice b) rejoyce	**Answer** a) rejoice

Letter Patterns: oi, oy
Quiz-Quiz-Trade

Instructions: Copy enough cards so each student has one card. Cut on dotted lines and fold in half.

Letter Patterns: oi, oy	Letter Patterns: oi, oy
Question Say the word. Which way looks right? **a) moist** **b) moyst**	**Answer** **a) moist**
Question Say the word. Which way looks right? **a) oyl** **b) oil**	**Answer** **b) oil**
Question Say the word. Which way looks right? **a) spoyl** **b) spoil**	**Answer** **b) spoil**
Question Say the word. Which way looks right? **a) point** **b) poynt**	**Answer** **a) point**

Letter Patterns: oi, oy
Quiz-Quiz-Trade

Instructions: Copy enough cards so each student has one card. Cut on dotted lines and fold in half.

Letter Patterns: oi, oy	Letter Patterns: oi, oy
Question Say the word. Which way looks right? **a) enjoy** **b) enjoi**	**Answer** **a) enjoy**

Letter Patterns: oi, oy	Letter Patterns: oi, oy
Question Say the word. Which way looks right? **a) joiful** **b) joyful**	**Answer** **b) joyful**

Letter Patterns: oi, oy	Letter Patterns: oi, oy
Question Say the word. Which way looks right? **a) voyage** **b) voiage**	**Answer** **a) voyage**

Letter Patterns: oi, oy	Letter Patterns: oi, oy
Question Say the word. Which way looks right? **a) cowboi** **b) cowboy**	**Answer** **b) cowboy**

Letter Patterns: oi, oy
Quiz-Quiz-Trade

Instructions: Copy enough cards so each student has one card. Cut on dotted lines and fold in half.

Letter Patterns: oi, oy

Question

Say the word.
Which way looks right?

a) roial
b) royal

Letter Patterns: oi, oy

Answer

b) royal

Letter Patterns: oi, oy

Question

Say the word.
Which way looks right?

a) oyster
b) oister

Letter Patterns: oi, oy

Answer

a) oyster

Letter Patterns: oi, oy

Question

Say the word.
Which way looks right?

a) soibean
b) soybean

Letter Patterns: oi, oy

Answer

b) soybean

Letter Patterns: oi, oy

Question

Say the word.
Which way looks right?

a) loial
b) loyal

Letter Patterns: oi, oy

Answer

b) loyal

Letter Patterns: oi, oy
Quiz-Quiz-Trade

Instructions: Copy enough cards so each student has one card. Cut on dotted lines and fold in half.

Letter Patterns: oi, oy

Question

Say the word.
Which way looks right?

a) toybox
b) toibox

Letter Patterns: oi, oy

Answer

a) toybox

Letter Patterns: oi, oy

Question

Say the word.
Which way looks right?

a) ploy
b) ploi

Letter Patterns: oi, oy

Answer

a) ploy

Letter Patterns: oi, oy

Question

Say the word.
Which way looks right?

a) decoi
b) decoy

Letter Patterns: oi, oy

Answer

b) decoy

Letter Patterns: oi, oy

Question

Say the word.
Which way looks right?

a) annoy
b) annoi

Letter Patterns: oi, oy

Answer

a) annoy

Letter Patterns: oi, oy
Quiz-Quiz-Trade

Instructions: Copy enough cards so each student has one card. Cut on dotted lines and fold in half.

Letter Patterns: oi, oy	Letter Patterns: oi, oy
Question Say the word. Which way looks right? **a) oink** **b) oynk**	**Answer** **a) oink**
Question Say the word. Which way looks right? **a) coil** **b) coyl**	**Answer** **a) coil**
Question Say the word. Which way looks right? **a) destroi** **b) destroy**	**Answer** **b) destroy**
Question Say the word. Which way looks right? **a) coyn** **b) coin**	**Answer** **b) coin**

Letter Patterns: au, aw
Quiz-Quiz-Trade

Instructions: Copy enough cards so each student has one card. Cut on dotted lines and fold in half.

Letter Patterns: au, aw **Question** Say the word. Which way looks right? **a) taught** **b) tawght**	**Letter Patterns: au, aw** **Answer** **a) taught**
Letter Patterns: au, aw **Question** Say the word. Which way looks right? **a) Paul** **b) Pawl**	**Letter Patterns: au, aw** **Answer** **a) Paul**
Letter Patterns: au, aw **Question** Say the word. Which way looks right? **a) awtumn** **b) autumn**	**Letter Patterns: au, aw** **Answer** **b) autumn**
Letter Patterns: au, aw **Question** Say the word. Which way looks right? **a) Awgust** **b) August**	**Letter Patterns: au, aw** **Answer** **b) August**

Letter Patterns: au, aw
Quiz-Quiz-Trade

Instructions: Copy enough cards so each student has one card. Cut on dotted lines and fold in half.

Letter Patterns: au, aw	Letter Patterns: au, aw
Question Say the word. Which way looks right? **a) dawghter** **b) daughter**	**Answer** **b) daughter**
Question Say the word. Which way looks right? **a) awtomobile** **b) automobile**	**Answer** **b) automobile**
Question Say the word. Which way looks right? **a) caught** **b) cawght**	**Answer** **a) caught**
Question Say the word. Which way looks right? **a) Drauing** **b) Drawing**	**Answer** **b) Drawing**

Letter Patterns: au, aw
Quiz-Quiz-Trade

Instructions: Copy enough cards so each student has one card. Cut on dotted lines and fold in half.

Letter Patterns: au, aw	Letter Patterns: au, aw
Question Say the word. Which way looks right? **a) laun** **b) lawn**	**Answer** **b) lawn**
Question Say the word. Which way looks right? **a) paw** **b) pau**	**Answer** **a) paw**
Question Say the word. Which way looks right? **a) awning** **b) auning**	**Answer** **a) awning**
Question Say the word. Which way looks right? **a) yaun** **b) yawn**	**Answer** **b) yawn**

Balanced Literacy • Third Grade • Skidmore & Graber
Kagan Publishing • 1 (800) 933-2667 • www.KaganOnline.com

Letter Patterns: au, aw
Quiz-Quiz-Trade

Instructions: Copy enough cards so each student has one card. Cut on dotted lines and fold in half.

Letter Patterns: au, aw	Letter Patterns: au, aw
Question Say the word. Which way looks right? a) hawk b) hauk	**Answer** a) hawk
Question Say the word. Which way looks right? a) claus b) claws	**Answer** b) claws
Question Say the word. Which way looks right? a) sau b) saw	**Answer** b) saw
Question Say the word. Which way looks right? a) crawl b) craul	**Answer** a) crawl

Letter Patterns: au, aw
Quiz-Quiz-Trade

Instructions: Copy enough cards so each student has one card. Cut on dotted lines and fold in half.

Letter Patterns: au, aw	Letter Patterns: au, aw
Question Say the word. Which way looks right? **a) haul** **b) hawl**	**Answer** **a) haul**
Question Say the word. Which way looks right? **a) laundry** **b) lawndry**	**Answer** **a) laundry**
Question Say the word. Which way looks right? **a) jau** **b) jaw**	**Answer** **b) jaw**
Question Say the word. Which way looks right? **a) sawdust** **b) saudust**	**Answer** **a) sawdust**

Letter Patterns: au, aw
Quiz-Quiz-Trade

Instructions: Copy enough cards so each student has one card. Cut on dotted lines and fold in half.

Letter Patterns: au, aw	Letter Patterns: au, aw
Question Say the word. Which way looks right? a) awthor b) author	**Answer** b) author
Question Say the word. Which way looks right? a) law b) lau	**Answer** a) law
Question Say the word. Which way looks right? a) hauls b) hawls	**Answer** a) hauls
Question Say the word. Which way looks right? a) autograph b) awtograph	**Answer** a) autograph

Letter Patterns: au, aw
Quiz-Quiz-Trade

Instructions: Copy enough cards so each student has one card. Cut on dotted lines and fold in half.

Letter Patterns: au, aw **Question** Say the word. Which way looks right? a) gnaws b) gnaus	**Letter Patterns: au, aw** **Answer** a) gnaws
Letter Patterns: au, aw **Question** Say the word. Which way looks right? a) astronawt b) astronaut	**Letter Patterns: au, aw** **Answer** b) astronaut
Letter Patterns: au, aw **Question** Say the word. Which way looks right? a) shaul b) shawl	**Letter Patterns: au, aw** **Answer** b) shawl
Letter Patterns: au, aw **Question** Say the word. Which way looks right? a) outlaws b) outlaus	**Letter Patterns: au, aw** **Answer** a) outlaws

Letter Patterns: ou, ow
Quiz-Quiz-Trade

Instructions: Copy enough cards so each student has one card. Cut on dotted lines and fold in half.

Letter Patterns: ou, ow

Question

Say the word.
Which way looks right?

a) bound
b) bownd

Letter Patterns: ou, ow

Answer

a) bound

Letter Patterns: ou, ow

Question

Say the word.
Which way looks right?

a) couch
b) cowch

Letter Patterns: ou, ow

Answer

a) couch

Letter Patterns: ou, ow

Question

Say the word.
Which way looks right?

a) flowr
b) flour

Letter Patterns: ou, ow

Answer

b) flour

Letter Patterns: ou, ow

Question

Say the word.
Which way looks right?

a) devowr
b) devour

Letter Patterns: ou, ow

Answer

b) devour

Letter Patterns: ou, ow
Quiz-Quiz-Trade

Instructions: Copy enough cards so each student has one card. Cut on dotted lines and fold in half.

Letter Patterns: ou, ow

Question

Say the word.
Which way looks right?

a) compownd
b) compound

Letter Patterns: ou, ow

Answer

b) compound

Letter Patterns: ou, ow

Question

Say the word.
Which way looks right?

a) amount
b) amownt

Letter Patterns: ou, ow

Answer

a) amount

Letter Patterns: ou, ow

Question

Say the word.
Which way looks right?

a) out
b) owt

Letter Patterns: ou, ow

Answer

a) out

Letter Patterns: ou, ow

Question

Say the word.
Which way looks right?

a) sownd
b) sound

Letter Patterns: ou, ow

Answer

b) sound

Letter Patterns: ou, ow
Quiz-Quiz-Trade

Instructions: Copy enough cards so each student has one card. Cut on dotted lines and fold in half.

Letter Patterns: ou, ow	Letter Patterns: ou, ow
Question Say the word. Which way looks right? **a) ground** **b) grownd**	**Answer** **a) ground**
Question Say the word. Which way looks right? **a) scout** **b) scowt**	**Answer** **a) scout**
Question Say the word. Which way looks right? **a) sprowt** **b) sprout**	**Answer** **b) sprout**
Question Say the word. Which way looks right? **a) pownce** **b) pounce**	**Answer** **b) pounce**

Letter Patterns: ou, ow
Quiz-Quiz-Trade

Instructions: Copy enough cards so each student has one card. Cut on dotted lines and fold in half.

Letter Patterns: ou, ow	Letter Patterns: ou, ow
Question Say the word. Which way looks right? **a) crown** **b) croun**	**Answer** **a) crown**
Question Say the word. Which way looks right? **a) pouder** **b) powder**	**Answer** **b) powder**
Question Say the word. Which way looks right? **a) crowd** **b) croud**	**Answer** **a) crowd**
Question Say the word. Which way looks right? **a) proul** **b) prowl**	**Answer** **b) prowl**

Letter Patterns: ou, ow
Quiz-Quiz-Trade

Instructions: Copy enough cards so each student has one card. Cut on dotted lines and fold in half.

Letter Patterns: ou, ow	Letter Patterns: ou, ow
Question Say the word. Which way looks right? **a) oul** **b) owl**	**Answer** **b) owl**

Letter Patterns: ou, ow	Letter Patterns: ou, ow
Question Say the word. Which way looks right? **a) clown** **b) cloun**	**Answer** **a) clown**

Letter Patterns: ou, ow	Letter Patterns: ou, ow
Question Say the word. Which way looks right? **a) groul** **b) growl**	**Answer** **b) growl**

Letter Patterns: ou, ow	Letter Patterns: ou, ow
Question Say the word. Which way looks right? **a) nou** **b) now**	**Answer** **b) now**

Letter Patterns: ou, ow
Quiz-Quiz-Trade

Instructions: Copy enough cards so each student has one card. Cut on dotted lines and fold in half.

Letter Patterns: ou, ow	Letter Patterns: ou, ow
Question Say the word. Which way looks right? **a) shouer** **b) shower**	**Answer** **b) shower**
Letter Patterns: ou, ow	Letter Patterns: ou, ow
Question Say the word. Which way looks right? **a) froun** **b) frown**	**Answer** **b) frown**
Letter Patterns: ou, ow	Letter Patterns: ou, ow
Question Say the word. Which way looks right? **a) towel** **b) touel**	**Answer** **a) towel**
Letter Patterns: ou, ow	Letter Patterns: ou, ow
Question Say the word. Which way looks right? **a) dounhill** **b) downhill**	**Answer** **b) downhill**

Letter Patterns: ou, ow
Quiz-Quiz-Trade

Instructions: Copy enough cards so each student has one card. Cut on dotted lines and fold in half.

Letter Patterns: ou, ow	Letter Patterns: ou, ow
Question Say the word. Which way looks right? a) hometoun b) hometown	**Answer** b) hometown
Question Say the word. Which way looks right? a) clowds b) clouds	**Answer** b) clouds
Question Say the word. Which way looks right? a) clubhowse b) clubhouse	**Answer** b) clubhouse
Question Say the word. Which way looks right? a) fountain b) fowntain	**Answer** a) fountain

Coach Me

Three different types of word study RallyCoach activities are provided: 1) cube, 2) spinner, and 3) sorting mat. Using the materials provided, one partner completes the task while the other is the coach. They switch roles for each new problem.

Activity Steps

STRUCTURE
RallyCoach

1. Depending on the activity below, each pair receives either a cube and a worksheet, a spinner and a worksheet, or a sorting mat and word cards.

2. First Partner A completes the task.
   - Cube: Partner rolls cube and uses result to fill in worksheet.
   - Spinner: Partner spins spinner and uses result to fill in worksheet.
   - Sorting Mat: Partner picks a word card and sorts it on the mat.

3. Partner B watches and listens, checks, and praises.

4. Then, Partner B rolls the cube, spins the spinner, or selects the next word card. Partner B completes the next problem.

5. Partner A watches and listens, checks, and praises.

6. The process continues until they complete their worksheet or sort all word cards.

Blacklines

Prefix (mis- and pre-) Cube

RallyCoach

Instructions: Copy the cube pattern onto cardstock for each pair. Cut out, fold, and tape together to form a cube. Partners take turns rolling the cube. The student rolling the cube chooses one incomplete word on the worksheet to make a word.

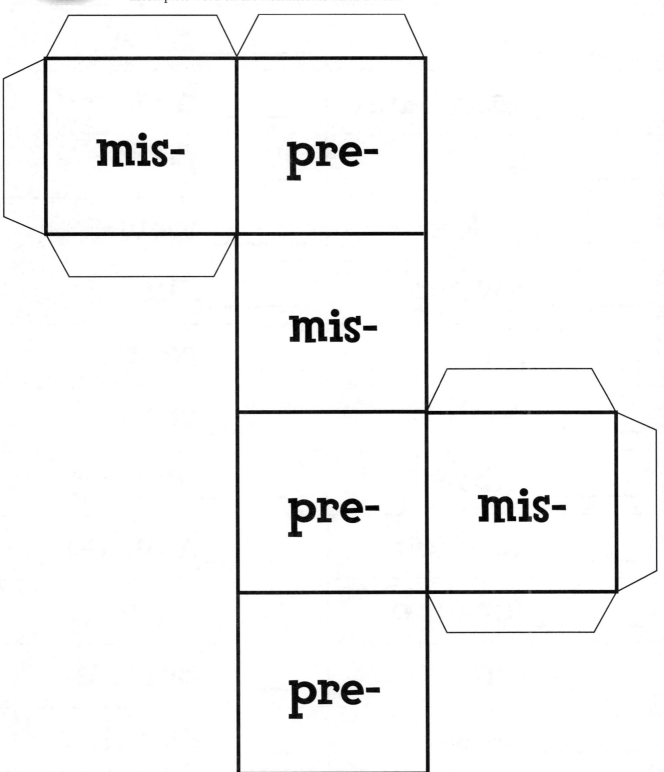

Prefix (mis- and pre-) Worksheet
RallyCoach

Instructions: Partners use worksheet with prefix cube.

_____take	_____chief
_____calculate	_____historic
_____tend	_____fit
_____judge	_____view
_____giving	_____fix
_____pay	_____read
_____spell	_____cook
_____inform	_____place
_____caution	_____handle
_____fortune	_____date
_____school	_____behave
_____test	_____match

Suffix (-less and -ness) Cube
RallyCoach

Instructions: Copy the cube pattern onto cardstock for each pair. Cut out, fold, and tape together to form a cube. Partners take turns rolling the cube. The student rolling the cube chooses one incomplete word on the worksheet to make a word.

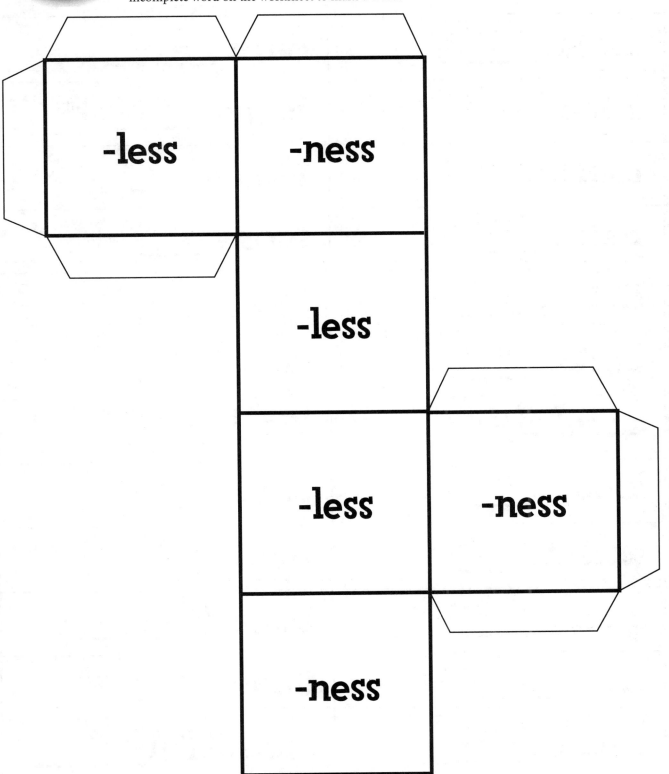

-less

-ness

-less

-less   -ness

-ness

Suffix (-less and -ness) Worksheet

RallyCoach

Instructions: Partners use worksheet with suffix cube.

seam_____	dark_____
wire_____	home_____
useful_____	thank_____
pain_____	score_____
hair_____	loud_____
taste_____	sad_____
careful_____	kind_____
loud_____	care_____
willing_____	help_____
good_____	breath_____
sleep_____	time_____
tender_____	forgetful_____

 Balanced Literacy • Third Grade • Skidmore & Graber
Kagan Publishing • 1 (800) 933-2667 • www.KaganOnline.com

Antonym-Synonym Cube
RallyCoach

Instructions: Copy the cube pattern onto cardstock for each pair. Cut out, fold, and tape to form a cube. Partners take turns rolling the cube. The student rolling the cube chooses a pair of words on the worksheet that fits the description "antonyms" or "synonyms."

synonyms **antonyms**

synonyms

antonyms **synonyms**

antonyms

Antonym-Synonym Worksheet

RallyCoach

Instructions: Partners use worksheet with Antonym-Synonym Cube. Write *A* if the word pair are antonyms. Write *S* if the word pair are synonyms.

unknown — famous _____	destroy — ruin _____
country — city _____	destroy — create _____
gaze — stare _____	sleep — snooze _____
repair — fix _____	laugh — sob _____
always — never _____	hide — disguise _____
giant — huge _____	noisy — quiet _____
pieces — parts _____	simple — difficult _____
friend — pal _____	exit — depart _____
straight — bent _____	friend — enemy _____
tight — loose _____	flame — fire _____
rocks — stones _____	laugh — giggle _____

Spinner (er, ir, ur)
RallyCoach

Instructions: Copy the spinner onto cardstock for each pair. Add a plastic/metal spinner in the middle or use a spinner made from a paper clip and a pencil. (To make a paper clip spinner: Place a paper clip over the center of the spinner. Place the pencil point on the center point of the spinner, through the paper clip. Using the other hand, spin the paper clip around the pencil point.) Partners take turns spinning. The student spinning chooses an incomplete word on the worksheet to form a word.

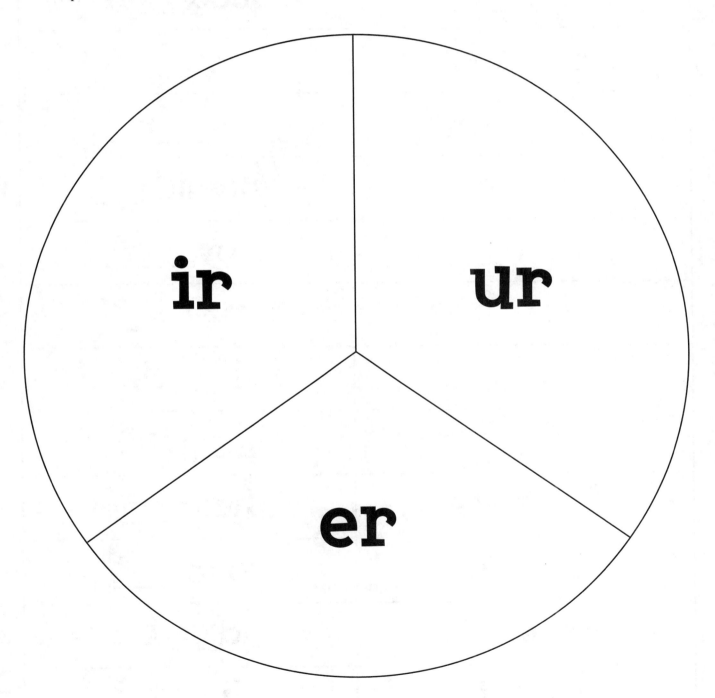

Worksheet (er, ir, ur)
RallyCoach

Instructions: Partners use worksheet with Spinner (er, ir, ur).

g_ _l	mod_ _n
p_ _son	s_ _
diff_ _ent	b_ _n
b_ _d	rememb_ _
moth_ _	ov_ _
t_ _n	nev_ _
h_ _	f_ _st
f_ _	_ _gent
f_ _nace	help_ _
th_ _d	conc_ _t
lett_ _	d_ _t
sh_ _t	h_ _t

Contraction Spinner
RallyCoach

Instructions: Copy the spinner onto cardstock for each pair. Add a plastic/metal spinner in the middle or use a spinner made from a paper clip and a pencil. (To make a paper clip spinner: Place a paper clip over the center of the spinner. Place the pencil point on the center point of the spinner, through the paper clip. Using the other hand, spin the paper clip around the pencil point.) Partners take turns spinning. The student spinning uses the word indicated by the spin and one word from the worksheet to make a contraction.

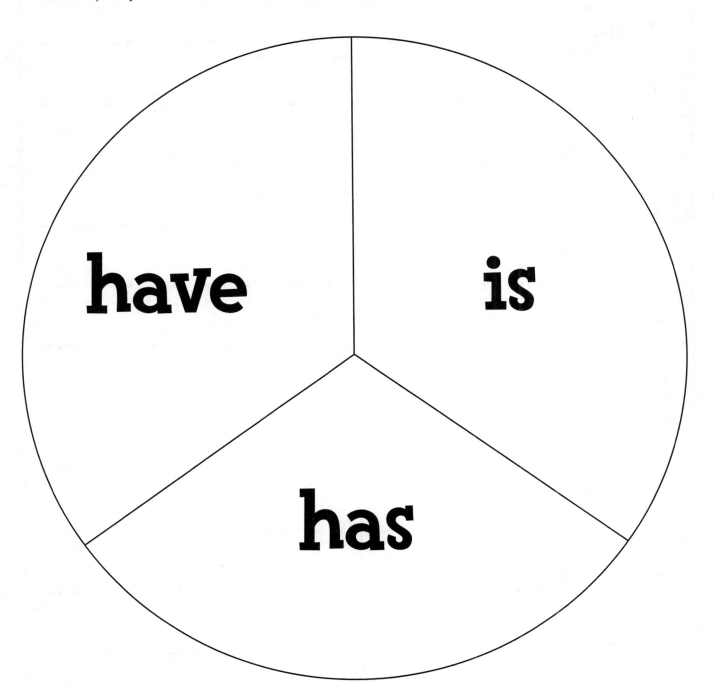

Contraction Worksheet
RallyCoach

Instructions: Partners use worksheet with Contraction Spinner. Partners write word from Spinner in first column. The two words are written as a contraction in the second column.

Word from Spinner	Contraction
could _____	_____
I _____	_____
should _____	_____
he _____	_____
here _____	_____
what _____	_____
she _____	_____
would _____	_____
it _____	_____
where _____	_____
you _____	_____
that _____	_____

 Balanced Literacy • Third Grade • Skidmore & Graber
Kagan Publishing • 1 (800) 933-2667 • www.KaganOnline.com

Forming Plurals Spinner
RallyCoach

Instructions: Copy the spinner onto cardstock for each pair. Add a plastic/metal spinner in the middle or use a spinner made from a paper clip and a pencil. (To make a paper clip spinner: Place a paper clip over the center of the spinner. Place the pencil point on the center point of the spinner, through the paper clip. Using the other hand, spin the paper clip around the pencil point.) Partners take turns spinning. The student spinning follows the direction indicated by the spin and applies it to one word from the worksheet to form a plural word.

add *es*   add *s*

change *y* to *i* and add *es*

Forming Plurals Worksheet
RallyCoach

Instructions: Partners use worksheet with Plurals Spinner.

candy _____	wish _____
house _____	school _____
glass _____	match _____
story _____	fly _____
bow _____	peach _____
city _____	brush _____
friend _____	family _____
dress _____	apple _____
baby _____	sky _____
fox _____	paper _____
pencil _____	tiger _____
cross _____	lunch _____

Adding s or es Sorting Mat
RallyCoach

Instructions: Copy one mat for each pair. Choose a word card. Add *s* or *es* to the word and write it in the correct column.

Add s	Add es

Adding *s* or *es* Word Cards
RallyCoach

Instructions: Copy one set of cards for each pair. Cut apart.

Word Cards	Word Cards
inch	tree
arch	hiss
fox	ax
bus	fish
fizz	crab
wish	bush
key	boy
dish	buzz
desk	glass
match	lunch
can	box
class	apple

Adding *s* or *es* Word Cards

RallyCoach

Instructions: Copy one set of cards for each pair. Cut apart.

Word Cards	Word Cards
lynx	success
rhinoceros	walrus
vanish	doctor
actress	crutch
cucumber	hourglass
swoosh	hairbrush
cross	bicycle
business	eyeglass
subject	embarrass
cockroach	telephone
taxicab	gash
ocean	hamburger

Adding *s* or *es* Word Cards
RallyCoach

Instructions: Copy one set of cards for each pair. Cut apart.

Word Cards	
cheese	canvas
lunchbox	market
virus	luncheon
splotch	circus
mattress	frizz
crouch	object
coach	torch
canvas	pedal
minute	champion
ditch	thickness
sandwich	minute
toothbrush	illness

Hard *c* or Soft *c* Sorting Mat
RallyCoach

Instructions: Copy one mat for each pair. Sort each word into the correct column according to the sound the *c* makes in the word.

Hard c Sound /k/	Soft c Sound /s/

Hard *c* or Soft *c* Word Cards

RallyCoach

Instructions: Copy one set of cards for each pair. Cut apart.

Word Cards		Word Cards	
	cub		came
	cell		color
	coin		camp
	cave		corner
	can		carrot
	cut		cook
	cow		city
	center		call
	cup		cake
	cone		cabin
	cool		come
	cents		cage

Hard *c* or Soft *c* Word Cards
RallyCoach

Instructions: Copy one set of cards for each pair. Cut apart.

Word Cards	Word Cards
cider	cottage
cartoon	calendar
camera	code
coastline	cease
coyote	community
cereal	curious
cement	caribou
correct	center
compound	carriage
cellar	careful
carousel	central
cylinder	celebrate

Hard *c* or Soft *c* Word Cards
RallyCoach

Instructions: Copy one set of cards for each pair. Cut apart.

Word Cards	Word Cards
caboose	college
cafeteria	carpenter
cymbal	cabbage
celebration	centimeter
citizen	cauliflower
coffee	celery
commercial	caravan
ceiling	catalog
castle	Cindy
camouflage	comedy
centipede	cinnamon
complete	collar

Hard *c* or Soft *c* Word Cards
RallyCoach

Instructions: Copy one set of cards for each pair. Cut apart.

Word Cards	Word Cards
space	camper
fancy	cricket
second	dance
icy	spicy
cigar	race
recess	corn
price	climb
club	mice
centimeter	juice
slice	centipede
cannot	once
since	brace

Words with *ea* Sorting Mat

RallyCoach

Instructions: Copy one mat for each pair. Write each *ea* word in the correct column. (Some words may go in two columns.)

ēa	ĕa	Different Sound

Balanced Literacy • Third Grade • Skidmore & Graber
Kagan Publishing • 1 (800) 933-2667 • www.KaganOnline.com

Words with *ea* Word Cards

RallyCoach

Instructions: Copy one set of cards for each pair. Cut apart.

Word Cards	Word Cards
beach	bear
oatmeal	beaver
bead	creature
bread	dead
east	measles
dreadful	breath
wheat	peacock
lead	disease
healthy	dreamy
cream	head
freak	beagle
bean	beautiful

Words with *ea* Word Cards

RallyCoach

Instructions: Copy one set of cards for each pair. Cut apart.

Word Cards		Word Cards	
greatness		earth	
reach		healed	
great		headache	
year		thread	
each		speak	
feather		deaf	
clean		heated	
eaten		meat	
pear		gear	
cheat		leaf	
cleaner		steak	
eagle		meant	

Words with *ea* Word Cards

RallyCoach

Instructions: Copy one set of cards for each pair. Cut apart.

Word Cards		Word Cards	
	please		teacher
	beneath		heavy
	heaven		meadow
	beam		threat
	breakfast		speak
	steal		beautiful
	peaches		zeal
	tear		wealth
	leather		sweater
	already		jealous
	cleanser		streak
	meaner		weapon

Rare Singulars/Plurals Sorting Mat

RallyCoach

Instructions: Copy one mat for each pair. Sort each word into the singulars or plurals column. (Some words may go in both columns.)

Singular Words (1)	Plural Words (2 or more)

Rare Singulars/Plurals
Word Cards

RallyCoach

Instructions: Copy one set of cards for each pair. Cut apart.

Word Cards	Word Cards
teeth	sheep
feet	deer
woman	ox
tooth	louse
children	men
tuna	goose
mouse	man
fish	moose
lice	child
women	student
foot	oxen
mice	geese

Activity

Word Study Showdown

Teams play Showdown to practice prefixes, suffixes, antonyms, synonyms, and homophones.

Activity Steps

STRUCTURE

Showdown

1. Each team receives a Team Set of cards and every student receives a Student Set of cards.

2. The Team Set is placed facedown in the middle of the team. Students hold their Student Set in their hands.

3. The teacher selects one student to be the Showdown Captain for the first round.

4. The Showdown Captain selects the top card from the middle and reads it aloud.

5. Working alone, students individually identify an answer from their card set.

6. When finished, teammates signal they are ready.

7. The Showdown Captain calls, "Showdown!"

8. Teammates show their answers at the same time.

9. The Showdown Captain leads checking.

10. If correct, the team celebrates. If not, the teammates coach, then celebrate.

11. The person to the left of the Showdown Captain becomes the Showdown Captain for the next round.

Blacklines

Prefixes: mis-, pre-
Showdown (Team Set)

Instructions: Copy one set of cards for each team. Cut apart.

Prefixes: mis-, pre- Team Set ____ view	Prefixes: mis-, pre- Team Set ____ match	Prefixes: mis-, pre- Team Set ____ take
Prefixes: mis-, pre- Team Set ____ school	Prefixes: mis-, pre- Team Set ____ test	Prefixes: mis-, pre- Team Set ____ pay
Prefixes: mis-, pre- Team Set ____ spell	Prefixes: mis-, pre- Team Set ____ handle	Prefixes: mis-, pre- Team Set ____ inform

Prefixes: mis-, pre-
Showdown (Team Set)

Instructions: Copy one set of cards for each pair. Cut apart.

Prefixes: mis-, pre- Team Set	Prefixes: mis-, pre- Team Set	Prefixes: mis-, pre- Team Set
____ giving	____ behave	____ understood
____ historic	____ place	____ heat
____ cook	____ fortune	____ caution

Prefixes: mis-, pre-
Showdown (Student Set)

Note: This page has cards for four students (one team). Copy, cut apart, and give each student one "mis-" and one "pre-" card.

Prefixes: mis-, pre- Student Set	Prefixes: mis-, pre- Student Set	Prefixes: mis-, pre- Student Set	Prefixes: mis-, pre- Student Set
mis-	**pre-**	**mis-**	**pre-**

Prefixes: mis-, pre- Student Set	Prefixes: mis-, pre- Student Set	Prefixes: mis-, pre- Student Set	Prefixes: mis-, pre- Student Set
mis-	**pre-**	**mis-**	**pre-**

Suffixes: -less, -ness

Showdown (Team Set)

Instructions: Copy one set of cards for each team. Cut apart.

thank ___	loud ___	home ___
hair ___	time ___	good ___
seam ___	kind ___	taste ___

Suffixes: -less, -ness Team Set (repeated on each card)

Balanced Literacy • Third Grade • Skidmore & Graber
Kagan Publishing • 1 (800) 933-2667 • www.KaganOnline.com

Suffixes: -less, -ness

Showdown (Team Set)

Instructions: Copy one set of cards for each team. Cut apart.

Suffixes: -less, -ness Team Set — **sad___**	Suffixes: -less, -ness Team Set — **help___**	Suffixes: -less, -ness Team Set — **tender___**
Suffixes: -less, -ness Team Set — **score___**	Suffixes: -less, -ness Team Set — **pain___**	Suffixes: -less, -ness Team Set — **care___**
Suffixes: -less, -ness Team Set — **dark___**	Suffixes: -less, -ness Team Set — **sleep___**	Suffixes: -less, -ness Team Set — **wire___**

Suffixes: -less, -ness
Showdown (Student Set)

Note: This page has cards for four students (one team). Copy, cut apart, and give each student one "-less" and one "-ness" card.

Suffixes: -less, -ness– Student Set	Suffixes: -less, -ness– Student Set	Suffixes: -less, -ness– Student Set	Suffixes: -less, -ness– Student Set
-less	**-ness**	**-less**	**-ness**

Suffixes: -less, -ness– Student Set	Suffixes: -less, -ness– Student Set	Suffixes: -less, -ness– Student Set	Suffixes: -less, -ness– Student Set
-less	**-ness**	**-less**	**-ness**

Antonyms, Synonyms, Homophones
Showdown (Team Set)

Instructions: Copy one set of cards for each team. Cut apart.

Antonyms, Synonyms, Homophones — Team Set	Antonyms, Synonyms, Homophones — Team Set	Antonyms, Synonyms, Homophones — Team Set
country city	**guest guessed**	**days daze**

Antonyms, Synonyms, Homophones — Team Set	Antonyms, Synonyms, Homophones — Team Set	Antonyms, Synonyms, Homophones — Team Set
lessen lesson	**bent straight**	**guide lead**

Antonyms, Synonyms, Homophones
Showdown (Team Set)

Instructions: Copy one set of cards for each team. Cut apart.

Antonyms, Synonyms, Homophones—Team Set	Antonyms, Synonyms, Homophones—Team Set	Antonyms, Synonyms, Homophones—Team Set
loud **noisy**	**way** **weigh**	**giggle** **laugh**
Antonyms, Synonyms, Homophones—Team Set	Antonyms, Synonyms, Homophones—Team Set	Antonyms, Synonyms, Homophones—Team Set
chews **choose**	**empty** **full**	**always** **never**

Antonyms, Synonyms, Homophones
Showdown (Team Set)

Instructions: Copy one set of cards for each team. Cut apart.

Antonyms, Synonyms, Homophones — Team Set	Antonyms, Synonyms, Homophones — Team Set	Antonyms, Synonyms, Homophones — Team Set
Knows nose	**berry bury**	**unknown strange**
Antonyms, Synonyms, Homophones — Team Set	Antonyms, Synonyms, Homophones — Team Set	Antonyms, Synonyms, Homophones — Team Set
hoarse horse	**ruin destroy**	**flour flower**

Antonyms, Synonyms, Homophones
Showdown (Team Set)

Instructions: Copy one set of cards for each team. Cut apart.

Antonyms, Synonyms, Homophones — Team Set	Antonyms, Synonyms, Homophones — Team Set	Antonyms, Synonyms, Homophones — Team Set
always forever	pause paws	capture catch
sob laugh	**simple easy**	**hurried busy**

Antonyms, Synonyms, Homophones
Showdown (Team Set)

Instructions: Copy one set of cards for each team. Cut apart.

Antonyms, Synonyms, Homophones—Team Set	Antonyms, Synonyms, Homophones—Team Set	Antonyms, Synonyms, Homophones—Team Set
wail **whale**	**pieces** **parts**	**scene** **seen**

Antonyms, Synonyms, Homophones—Team Set	Antonyms, Synonyms, Homophones—Team Set	Antonyms, Synonyms, Homophones—Team Set
freeze **melt**	**towed** **toad**	**bucket** **pail**

Antonyms, Synonyms, Homophones
Showdown (Team Set)

Instructions: Copy one set of cards for each team. Cut apart.

Antonyms, Synonyms,
Homophones — Team Set

**intelligent
smart**

Antonyms, Synonyms,
Homophones — Team Set

**remember
forget**

Antonyms, Synonyms,
Homophones — Team Set

**triumphant
victorious**

Antonyms, Synonyms,
Homophones — Team Set

**snooze
sleep**

Antonyms, Synonyms,
Homophones — Team Set

**clothes
close**

Antonyms, Synonyms,
Homophones — Team Set

**dye
die**

Antonyms, Synonyms, Homophones
Showdown (Team Set)

Instructions: Copy one set of cards for each team. Cut apart.

Antonyms, Synonyms, Homophones—Team Set
examine **study**

Antonyms, Synonyms, Homophones—Team Set
reign **rain**

Antonyms, Synonyms, Homophones—Team Set
failure **success**

Antonyms, Synonyms, Homophones—Team Set
certainly **definitely**

Antonyms, Synonyms, Homophones—Team Set
prints **prince**

Antonyms, Synonyms, Homophones—Team Set
rotate **turn**

Antonyms, Synonyms, Homophones
Showdown (Student Set)

Note: This page has cards for two students. Copy, cut apart, and give each student one set of cards.

Antonyms, Synonyms, Homophones—Student Set	Antonyms, Synonyms, Homophones—Student Set	Antonyms, Synonyms, Homophones—Student Set
antonyms	**synonyms**	**homophones**

Antonyms, Synonyms, Homophones—Student Set	Antonyms, Synonyms, Homophones—Student Set	Antonyms, Synonyms, Homophones—Student Set
antonyms	**synonyms**	**homophones**

Balanced Literacy • Third Grade • Skidmore & Graber
Kagan Publishing • 1 (800) 933-2667 • www.KaganOnline.com

Activity

Word Wall Spelling

After spelling the word themselves, teammates put their "heads together" to ensure all members can correctly spell the word wall word. The teacher then calls a number and all students with that number share their team's spelling.

STRUCTURE
Numbered Heads Together

Note:
The Word Wall Cards on the following pages are not used for this activity. They are provided for your convenience to post on your word wall. However, before you begin this activity, make sure you take down word wall words students will spell.

Activity Steps

1 Students number off in small groups.

2 Teacher reads a selected word from the Priority Word List.

3 Students privately write the word on a markerboard or on a piece of paper.

4 Teacher says, "Heads Together!" and students lift up from their chairs to put their heads together, show their answers, and discuss until they reach consensus on the word spelling.

5 Everyone clears their boards and sits down when they agree.

6 The teacher calls out a number. All students with that number write the agreed-upon spelling of the word on their markerboards.

7 All students with their number selected hold up their boards simultaneously. The teacher writes each group's spelling on the overhead.

8 The teacher leads the class in a discussion of each spelling by asking questions such as "Which way looks right?" "How do you know?" or "What was the tricky part or familiar part?"

9 Teammates celebrate or correct spelling on boards.

10 The process is repeated for each new word.

Note: "Additional Word Wall Words" provide extra word choices.

Blacklines

Third Grade Priority Word List
Numbered Heads Together

Instructions: Words to be used with Word Wall Spelling.

a	but	good	left	number	set	time	with
about	by	great	like	of	she	to	words
after	called	had	line	off	should	too	work
again	came	has	little	old	small	two	would
air	could	have	long	on	so	under	write
all	day	he	look	one	some	up	you
also	did	help	made	only	still	us	your
am	different	her	make	or	such	use	
an	do	here	man	other	take	very	
and	does	him	many	our	tell	was	
another	down	his	may	out	than	water	
any	each	home	me	over	that	way	
are	end	how	men	own	the	we	
around	even	I	more	part	their	well	
as	every	if	most	people	them	went	
at	find	in	much	place	then	were	
away	first	into	must	put	there	what	
back	for	is	my	read	these	when	
be	found	it	name	right	they	where	
because	from	its	never	said	think	which	
been	get	just	new	same	this	who	
between	give	know	not	say	three	why	
big	go	last	now	see	through	will	

Third Grade Priority Word Wall Cards

Instructions: Use the cards provided to create a Word Wall.

Third Grade Priority Word Wall Cards — **air**	Third Grade Priority Word Wall Cards — **all**	Third Grade Priority Word Wall Cards — **also**	Third Grade Priority Word Wall Cards — **am**
Third Grade Priority Word Wall Cards — **a**	Third Grade Priority Word Wall Cards — **about**	Third Grade Priority Word Wall Cards — **after**	Third Grade Priority Word Wall Cards — **again**

Third Grade Priority Word Wall Cards

Instructions: Use the cards provided to create a Word Wall.

Third Grade Priority Word Wall Cards

are

Third Grade Priority Word Wall Cards

around

Third Grade Priority Word Wall Cards

as

Third Grade Priority Word Wall Cards

at

Third Grade Priority Word Wall Cards

an

Third Grade Priority Word Wall Cards

and

Third Grade Priority Word Wall Cards

another

Third Grade Priority Word Wall Cards

any

Third Grade Priority
Word Wall Cards

Instructions: Use the cards provided to create a Word Wall.

Third Grade Priority Word Wall Cards **been**	Third Grade Priority Word Wall Cards **between**	Third Grade Priority Word Wall Cards **big**	Third Grade Priority Word Wall Cards **but**
Third Grade Priority Word Wall Cards **away**	Third Grade Priority Word Wall Cards **back**	Third Grade Priority Word Wall Cards **be**	Third Grade Priority Word Wall Cards **because**

Third Grade Priority Word Wall Cards

Instructions: Use the cards provided to create a Word Wall.

Third Grade Priority Word Wall Cards

day

Third Grade Priority Word Wall Cards

did

Third Grade Priority Word Wall Cards

different

Third Grade Priority Word Wall Cards

do

Third Grade Priority Word Wall Cards

by

Third Grade Priority Word Wall Cards

called

Third Grade Priority Word Wall Cards

came

Third Grade Priority Word Wall Cards

could

Third Grade Priority Word Wall Cards

Instructions: Use the cards provided to create a Word Wall.

Third Grade Priority Word Wall Cards

even

Third Grade Priority Word Wall Cards

every

Third Grade Priority Word Wall Cards

find

Third Grade Priority Word Wall Cards

first

Third Grade Priority Word Wall Cards

does

Third Grade Priority Word Wall Cards

down

Third Grade Priority Word Wall Cards

each

Third Grade Priority Word Wall Cards

end

Third Grade Priority
Word Wall Cards

Instructions: Use the cards provided to create a Word Wall.

Third Grade Priority Word Wall Cards	Third Grade Priority Word Wall Cards	Third Grade Priority Word Wall Cards	Third Grade Priority Word Wall Cards
give	go	good	great
for	found	from	get

Third Grade Priority Word Wall Cards

Instructions: Use the cards provided to create a Word Wall.

Third Grade Priority Word Wall Cards **help**	Third Grade Priority Word Wall Cards **her**	Third Grade Priority Word Wall Cards **here**	Third Grade Priority Word Wall Cards **him**
Third Grade Priority Word Wall Cards **had**	Third Grade Priority Word Wall Cards **has**	Third Grade Priority Word Wall Cards **have**	Third Grade Priority Word Wall Cards **he**

Third Grade Priority Word Wall Cards

Instructions: Use the cards provided to create a Word Wall.

Third Grade Priority Word Wall Cards

if

Third Grade Priority Word Wall Cards

in

Third Grade Priority Word Wall Cards

into

Third Grade Priority Word Wall Cards

is

Third Grade Priority Word Wall Cards

his

Third Grade Priority Word Wall Cards

home

Third Grade Priority Word Wall Cards

how

Third Grade Priority Word Wall Cards

I

Third Grade Priority Word Wall Cards

Instructions: Use the cards provided to create a Word Wall.

Third Grade Priority Word Wall Cards

last

Third Grade Priority Word Wall Cards

left

Third Grade Priority Word Wall Cards

like

Third Grade Priority Word Wall Cards

line

Third Grade Priority Word Wall Cards

it

Third Grade Priority Word Wall Cards

its

Third Grade Priority Word Wall Cards

just

Third Grade Priority Word Wall Cards

know

Third Grade Priority Word Wall Cards

Instructions: Use the cards provided to create a Word Wall.

Third Grade Priority Word Wall Cards

make

Third Grade Priority Word Wall Cards

man

Third Grade Priority Word Wall Cards

many

Third Grade Priority Word Wall Cards

may

Third Grade Priority Word Wall Cards

little

Third Grade Priority Word Wall Cards

long

Third Grade Priority Word Wall Cards

look

Third Grade Priority Word Wall Cards

made

Third Grade Priority
Word Wall Cards

Instructions: Use the cards provided to create a Word Wall.

Third Grade Priority Word Wall Cards — **much**

Third Grade Priority Word Wall Cards — **must**

Third Grade Priority Word Wall Cards — **my**

Third Grade Priority Word Wall Cards — **name**

Third Grade Priority Word Wall Cards — **me**

Third Grade Priority Word Wall Cards — **men**

Third Grade Priority Word Wall Cards — **more**

Third Grade Priority Word Wall Cards — **most**

Third Grade Priority
Word Wall Cards

Instructions: Use the cards provided to create a Word Wall.

Third Grade Priority Word Wall Cards

number

Third Grade Priority Word Wall Cards

of

Third Grade Priority Word Wall Cards

off

Third Grade Priority Word Wall Cards

old

Third Grade Priority Word Wall Cards

never

Third Grade Priority Word Wall Cards

new

Third Grade Priority Word Wall Cards

not

Third Grade Priority Word Wall Cards

now

Third Grade Priority
Word Wall Cards

Instructions: Use the cards provided to create a Word Wall.

Third Grade Priority Word Wall Cards

other

Third Grade Priority Word Wall Cards

our

Third Grade Priority Word Wall Cards

out

Third Grade Priority Word Wall Cards

over

Third Grade Priority Word Wall Cards

on

Third Grade Priority Word Wall Cards

one

Third Grade Priority Word Wall Cards

only

Third Grade Priority Word Wall Cards

or

Third Grade Priority
Word Wall Cards

Instructions: Use the cards provided to create a Word Wall.

Third Grade Priority Word Wall Cards

put

Third Grade Priority Word Wall Cards

read

Third Grade Priority Word Wall Cards

right

Third Grade Priority Word Wall Cards

said

Third Grade Priority Word Wall Cards

own

Third Grade Priority Word Wall Cards

part

Third Grade Priority Word Wall Cards

people

Third Grade Priority Word Wall Cards

place

Third Grade Priority
Word Wall Cards

Instructions: Use the cards provided to create a Word Wall.

Third Grade Priority Word Wall Cards

she

Third Grade Priority Word Wall Cards

should

Third Grade Priority Word Wall Cards

small

Third Grade Priority Word Wall Cards

so

Third Grade Priority Word Wall Cards

same

Third Grade Priority Word Wall Cards

say

Third Grade Priority Word Wall Cards

see

Third Grade Priority Word Wall Cards

set

Third Grade Priority Word Wall Cards

Instructions: Use the cards provided to create a Word Wall.

Third Grade Priority Word Wall Cards

tell

Third Grade Priority Word Wall Cards

than

Third Grade Priority Word Wall Cards

that

Third Grade Priority Word Wall Cards

the

Third Grade Priority Word Wall Cards

some

Third Grade Priority Word Wall Cards

still

Third Grade Priority Word Wall Cards

such

Third Grade Priority Word Wall Cards

take

Balanced Literacy • Third Grade • Skidmore & Graber
Kagan Publishing • 1 (800) 933-2667 • www.KaganOnline.com

Third Grade Priority
Word Wall Cards

Instructions: Use the cards provided to create a Word Wall.

Third Grade Priority Word Wall Cards — **these**	Third Grade Priority Word Wall Cards — **they**	Third Grade Priority Word Wall Cards — **think**	Third Grade Priority Word Wall Cards — **this**
Third Grade Priority Word Wall Cards — **their**	Third Grade Priority Word Wall Cards — **them**	Third Grade Priority Word Wall Cards — **then**	Third Grade Priority Word Wall Cards — **there**

Third Grade Priority
Word Wall Cards

Instructions: Use the cards provided to create a Word Wall.

Third Grade Priority Word Wall Cards

too

Third Grade Priority Word Wall Cards

two

Third Grade Priority Word Wall Cards

under

Third Grade Priority Word Wall Cards

up

Third Grade Priority Word Wall Cards

three

Third Grade Priority Word Wall Cards

through

Third Grade Priority Word Wall Cards

time

Third Grade Priority Word Wall Cards

to

Third Grade Priority Word Wall Cards

Instructions: Use the cards provided to create a Word Wall.

Third Grade Priority Word Wall Cards

water

Third Grade Priority Word Wall Cards

way

Third Grade Priority Word Wall Cards

we

Third Grade Priority Word Wall Cards

well

Third Grade Priority Word Wall Cards

us

Third Grade Priority Word Wall Cards

use

Third Grade Priority Word Wall Cards

very

Third Grade Priority Word Wall Cards

was

Third Grade Priority
Word Wall Cards

Instructions: Use the cards provided to create a Word Wall.

Third Grade Priority Word Wall Cards	Third Grade Priority Word Wall Cards	Third Grade Priority Word Wall Cards	Third Grade Priority Word Wall Cards
where	**which**	**who**	**why**
went	**were**	**what**	**when**

Third Grade Priority
Word Wall Cards

Instructions: Use the cards provided to create a Word Wall.

Third Grade Priority Word Wall Cards

would

Third Grade Priority Word Wall Cards

write

Third Grade Priority Word Wall Cards

you

Third Grade Priority Word Wall Cards

your

Third Grade Priority Word Wall Cards

will

Third Grade Priority Word Wall Cards

with

Third Grade Priority Word Wall Cards

words

Third Grade Priority Word Wall Cards

work

Third Grade Additional
Word Wall Cards

Instructions: Use the cards provided to create a Word Wall.

Third Grade Additional Word Wall Cards

above

Third Grade Additional Word Wall Cards

year

Third Grade Additional Word Wall Cards

night

Third Grade Additional Word Wall Cards

story

Third Grade Additional Word Wall Cards

always

Third Grade Additional Word Wall Cards

house

Third Grade Additional Word Wall Cards

important

Third Grade Additional Word Wall Cards

animal

Third Grade Additional Word Wall Cards

Instructions: Use the cards provided to create a Word Wall.

Third Grade Additional Word Wall Cards

half

Third Grade Additional Word Wall Cards

order

Third Grade Additional Word Wall Cards

remember

Third Grade Additional Word Wall Cards

brought

Third Grade Additional Word Wall Cards

near

Third Grade Additional Word Wall Cards

example

Third Grade Additional Word Wall Cards

money

Third Grade Additional Word Wall Cards

body

Third Grade Additional
Word Wall Cards

Instructions: Use the cards provided to create a Word Wall.

Third Grade Additional Word Wall Cards

earth

Third Grade Additional Word Wall Cards

picture

Third Grade Additional Word Wall Cards

since

Third Grade Additional Word Wall Cards

sentence

Third Grade Additional Word Wall Cards

while

Third Grade Additional Word Wall Cards

until

Third Grade Additional Word Wall Cards

life

Third Grade Additional Word Wall Cards

kind

Third Grade Additional Word Wall Cards

Instructions: Use the cards provided to create a Word Wall.

Third Grade Additional Word Wall Cards

thought

Third Grade Additional Word Wall Cards

world

Third Grade Additional Word Wall Cards

enough

Third Grade Additional Word Wall Cards

several

Third Grade Additional Word Wall Cards

young

Third Grade Additional Word Wall Cards

heard

Third Grade Additional Word Wall Cards

against

Third Grade Additional Word Wall Cards

close

Third Grade Additional Word Wall Cards

Instructions: Use the cards provided to create a Word Wall.

Third Grade Additional Word Wall Cards

country

Third Grade Additional Word Wall Cards

change

Third Grade Additional Word Wall Cards

turned

Third Grade Additional Word Wall Cards

second

Third Grade Additional Word Wall Cards

toward

Third Grade Additional Word Wall Cards

family

Third Grade Additional Word Wall Cards

ground

Third Grade Additional Word Wall Cards

nothing

Third Grade Additional
Word Wall Cards

Instructions: Use the cards provided to create a Word Wall.

Third Grade Additional Word Wall Cards

living

Third Grade Additional Word Wall Cards

really

Third Grade Additional Word Wall Cards

idea

Third Grade Additional Word Wall Cards

those

Third Grade Additional Word Wall Cards

whole

Third Grade Additional Word Wall Cards

across

Third Grade Additional Word Wall Cards

answer

Third Grade Additional Word Wall Cards

group

Third Grade Additional Word Wall Cards

Instructions: Use the cards provided to create a Word Wall.

Third Grade Additional Word Wall Cards

during

Third Grade Additional Word Wall Cards

usually

Third Grade Additional Word Wall Cards

learned

Third Grade Additional Word Wall Cards

asked

Third Grade Additional Word Wall Cards

school

Third Grade Additional Word Wall Cards

children

Third Grade Additional Word Wall Cards

once

Third Grade Blank
Word Wall Cards

Instructions: Use the cards to add additional words.

Third Grade Word Wall Cards

Third Grade Word Wall Cards

Third Grade Word Wall Cards

Third Grade Word Wall Cards

Third Grade Word Wall Cards

Third Grade Word Wall Cards

Third Grade Word Wall Cards

Third Grade Word Wall Cards

Fluency

Fluency

Fluency is a part of an effective reading program. When a reader is fluent, energies are automatically channeled into comprehending the text instead of decoding words.

Reading fluency includes the following components:
- expression (stress, pitch, volume, clarity)
- phrasing (pauses, word groups)
- rate (just the right speed)
- accuracy (correct words and punctuation)

The fluency resources and materials at the beginning of this section are designed to be used in the suggested order to scaffold the learner and ensure understanding (*aloud* and *shared*). The remainder of the activities in this section are designed to provide fluency practice (*guided* and *independent*).

Table of Fluency Resources

Page(s)	Resources	Balanced Literacy				
		Aloud	Shared	Guided	Independent	Literature Circles
360	Fluency Resource/Materials Descriptions					
361	Fluency Bookmarks	●	●	●	●	●
362	Fluency Graphics/Note Taking	●	●	●	●	●

Table of Fluency Activities

Page(s)	Activities	Blacklines	Balanced Literacy				
			Aloud	Shared	Guided	Independent	Literature Circles
364	**RallyCoach Activities**						
365	Expression	• Rubric and Graph	●	●	●	●	●
366	Phrasing	• Rubric and Graph	●	●	●	●	●
367	Accuracy	• Rubric and Graph	●	●	●	●	●
368	Rate	• Rubric and Graph	●	●	●	●	●
369	Fluency	• Continuum Worksheet	●	●	●	●	●
370	**Poems for Two Voices Activities**						
371	Homophones	• Copy of Poem		●	●		
372	Pilgrims	• Copy of Poem		●	●		
373	Comprehension Questions	• Copy of Poem		●	●		
374	Blank Form	• Blank Worksheet		●	●		
375	**RallyRobin Activity**						
376	Reading with Different Emotions	• Passage Cards • Emotion Cards		●	●	●	

Balanced Literacy • Third Grade • Skidmore & Graber
Kagan Publishing • 1 (800) 933-2667 • www.KaganOnline.com

Fluency Resources

Fluency Resources

Resources/Materials Descriptions

Fluency Bookmark (p. 361)
Fluency is automatic and accurate recognition of words in a text while using phrasing and expression in a way that makes reading sound like spoken language. The Fluency Bookmark is a visual prompting tool for students to use as they learn and practice the components of fluent reading.

Fluency Graphics/Note Taking (p. 362)
The fluency page provides flexible instructional uses. The teacher may have students attach their own labels, graphics, or notes to build mental connections as they become fluent readers.

Fluency Rubrics and Graphs (pp. 365–368)
The broad fluency components of expression, phrasing, rate, and accuracy have been defined through the rubric continuum to increase students' fluency knowledge, self-awareness, and monitoring of progress.

Students must be given opportunities to reread and practice if fluency is going to improve. The graph below each rubric provides students with a visual record for charting their own progress as they practice with a partner or individually.

Together, these two tools provide data for reflection and conversation between students and between student and teacher.

Fluency Continuum (p. 369)
After using the Rubrics and Graphs described above to create a solid understanding of fluency, the Fluency Continuum becomes another self-monitoring option for students.

Fluency Expression

expression
- stress
- pitch
- volume
- clarity

phrasing
- pauses
- word groups

rate
- speed (just right)

accuracy
- right words
- correct pronunciation

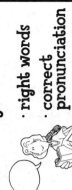

Fluency Expression

expression
- stress
- pitch
- volume
- clarity

phrasing
- pauses
- word groups

rate
- speed (just right)

accuracy
- right words
- correct pronunciation

Fluency Expression

expression
- stress
- pitch
- volume
- clarity

phrasing
- pauses
- word groups

rate
- speed (just right)

accuracy
- right words
- correct pronunciation

Fluency Expression

expression
- stress
- pitch
- volume
- clarity

phrasing
- pauses
- word groups

rate
- speed (just right)

accuracy
- right words
- correct pronunciation

Fluency Graphics/Note Taking

Instructions: Copy for each student.

Fluency Graphics/Note Taking	Fluency Graphics/Note Taking
expression  · stress · pitch · volume · clarity	

Fluency Graphics/Note Taking	Fluency Graphics/Note Taking
phrasing  · pauses · word groups	

Fluency Graphics/Note Taking	Fluency Graphics/Note Taking
rate  · speed (just right)	

Fluency Graphics/Note Taking	Fluency Graphics/Note Taking
accuracy  · right words · correct pronunciation	

Fluency Activities

Activity

Fluency Scoring

Students read a text passage to a partner. The partner uses a rubric to score the reading on one dimension. Students practice reading the same passage to improve their fluency and chart their progress.

Activity Steps

1. There are four rubrics provided to work on different dimensions of fluency. Each student receives a rubric sheet.

2. Partner A reads the text passage while Partner B listens carefully, paying special attention to the rubric scoring.

3. Partner B uses the rubric to score Partner A's reading. Partner B colors in the score in the "1st time" column of the graph. Then Partner B describes the score and how Partner A can improve.

4. Partner B then reads while Partner A listens.

5. Partner A scores the reading by filling in the graph and provides feedback to Partner B.

6. The process is repeated multiple times with the same text passage to improve fluency. There are 5 columns on the graph provided so students can graph their progress.

STRUCTURE
RallyCoach

Hint:
Tell students in advance that they will be scoring each other on their reading. The scores are used only as a way for students to provide each other constructive feedback and chart their progress.

Blacklines

Expression Rubric
RallyCoach

Instructions: Copy for each student.

Score	1	2	3	4
Expression • Stress • Pitch • Volume • Clarity	No Voice change	Voice changes sometimes	Voice changes most of the time when needed	Voice changes when needed

Expression Graph
RallyCoach

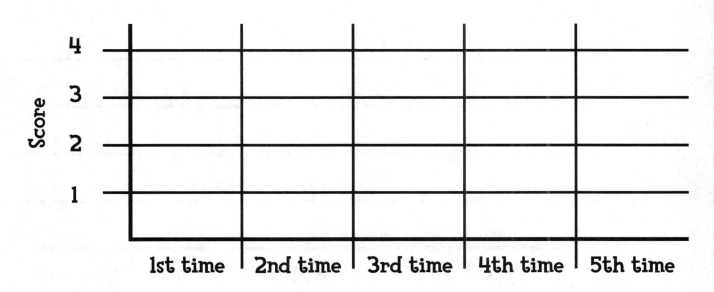

Name _____

Phrasing Rubric
RallyCoach

Instructions: Copy for each student.

Score	1	2	3	4
Phrasing • Pauses • Word Groups	Reads word by word and does not stop at punctuation	Reads in small chunks and sometimes stops at punctuation	Reads in larger chunks and usually stops at punctuation	Reads in long chunks and stops at punctuation

Phrasing Graph
RallyCoach

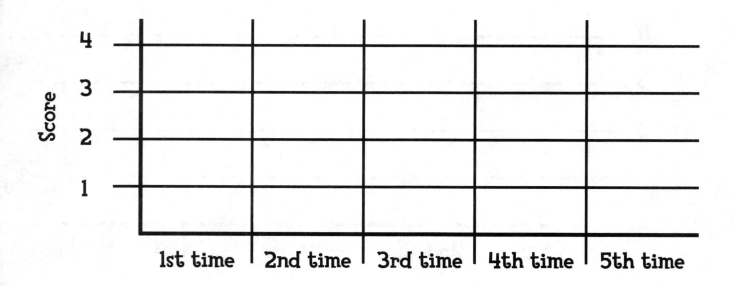

Name _____

Accuracy Rubric
RallyCoach

Instructions: Copy for each student.

Score	1	2	3	4
Accuracy • Right Words • Correct Pronunciation	Many errors	Errors, which sometimes change the meaning	Some errors, which do not change the meaning	Very few or no errors Words correctly pronounced

Accuracy Graph
RallyCoach

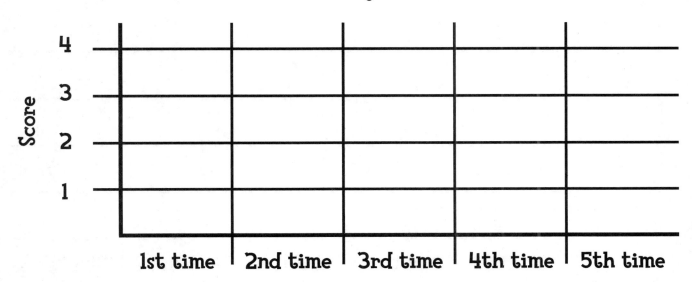

Name _____

Rate Rubric
RallyCoach

Instructions: Copy for each student.

Score	1	2	3	4
Rate • Speed (Just Right)	Reads too fast or too slow Hard to understand	Reads too fast or too slow sometimes	Reads "just right" most of the time	Keeps speed steady and "just right"

Rate Graph
RallyCoach

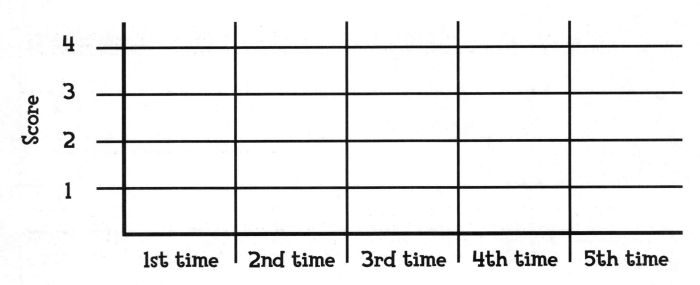

Name _____

Fluency Continuum
RallyCoach

Instructions: Copy for each student.

Fluency Continuum

expression

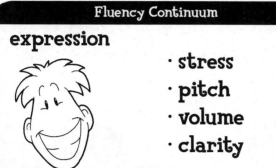

- stress
- pitch
- volume
- clarity

Fluency Continuum

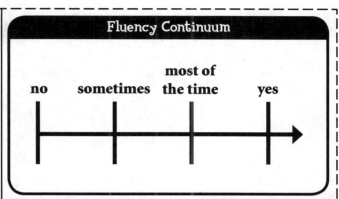

no   sometimes   most of the time   yes

Fluency Continuum

phrasing

- pauses
- word groups

Fluency Continuum

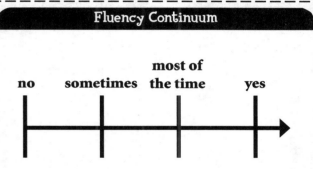

no   sometimes   most of the time   yes

Fluency Continuum

rate

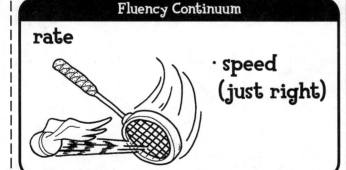

- speed (just right)

Fluency Continuum

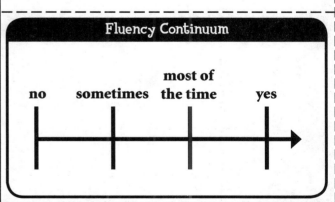

no   sometimes   most of the time   yes

Fluency Continuum

accuracy

- right words
- correct pronunciation

Fluency Continuum

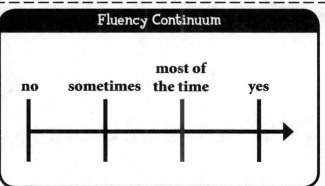

no   sometimes   most of the time   yes

Activities

Fluency Poems

Partners present a poem—recited at times by one partner, the other partner, or both.

Activity Steps

1 The teacher provides students a poem. The poem has some lines labeled "A," some lines labeled "B," and some lines labeled, "AB." The teacher assigns pairs.

2 Pairs practice their poems. Partner A reads the A lines. Partner B reads the B lines. They read the AB lines in unison. Students listen carefully to their partners to keep the flow.

3 When ready, pairs read their poem to another pair.

STRUCTURE
Poems for Two Voices

Blacklines

Homophones

Poems for Two Voices

Instructions: Copy for each student or pair.

A "Homophones" are words that sound the same but are <u>not</u> spelled the same.

B "Homo" means same. "Phone" can mean sound. When you talk on the telephone, you hear a voice.

A So..."homophone" means words that sound the same.

B blew – blue: The wind <u>blew</u> clouds across the <u>blue</u> sky.

A Know – no: I <u>know</u> my mom will say "<u>no</u>".

AB How will we know which way to write the word?

A We must think about what we know! We need to use our strategies.

B Oh, like the meaning of the word in a sentence?

A Yes! And when we write the word, we must try the word several ways to see which way looks right.

B I know another one! Think about the letter patterns.

A Think about where you've seen the word before.

AB Same sounding words like homophones shouldn't make you shutter and groan. Just think about the many strategies you have known.

Pilgrims

Poems for Two Voices

Instructions: Copy for each student or pair.

A Why did the Pilgrims come to America?

B The Pilgrims left their homeland in search of a place to live, where they would be free from the king telling them what church they had to attend.

A How did the Pilgrims get to America?

B One hundred and two Pilgrims boarded a ship called the *Mayflower* on August 5, 1620, for their journey from England to America.

A What did the Pilgrims take with them?

AB Not much! Whatever did not fit into a chest had to be left behind.

A What did the Pilgrims eat on the *Mayflower*?

B Day after day, they ate the same type of food—salted meat and hard, dry biscuits. Most of the days they ate cold food because the stormy weather made it dangerous to start a fire on the ship.

A How did the Pilgrims survive once they got to America?

B The Pilgrims met friendly Native Americans, who taught them how to fish, hunt, and plant gardens.

A How did the Pilgrims spend Thanksgiving?

B The Pilgrims and Native Americans played games, ate, and had fun together.

AB It was a time for sharing and giving thanks!

Comprehension Questions

Poems for Two Voices

Instructions: Copy for each student or pair.

A   Stopping to ask myself questions as I read

B   Is the best way to remember and recall

AB   Information that I might read

A   What is important to remember?

B   Is there anything I don't understand, such as...

A   How to pronounce a word or what a word means?

AB   All these questions will keep me involved, for sure!

A   My purpose for reading will keep me on track

B   As I stay focused and attentive

AB   My comprehension, it will not lack!

Blank Form

Poems for Two Voices

Names: _____

_____

Our Poem Is About: _____

Instructions: Copy for each pair of students.

A _____

B _____

A _____

B _____

AB _____

A _____

B _____

A _____

B _____

AB _____

Balanced Literacy • Third Grade • Skidmore & Graber
Kagan Publishing • 1 (800) 933-2667 • www.KaganOnline.com

Reading with Emotion

In pairs, students alternate reading text passages using different emotions indicated by emotion task cards.

STRUCTURE
RallyRobin

Note:
Copy the Emotion Cards and the Reading Passages Cards on different colors to keep the cards separate.

Activity Steps

1. Each pair receives a set of Reading Passages and a set of Emotion Cards. They create two stacks, facedown between them.

2. Partner A chooses an Emotion Card and a Reading Passage Card.

3. Partner A reads the Reading Passage Card using the emotion indicated on the Emotion Card.

4. Partner B encourages and praises.

5. Partner B chooses a different Emotion Card, but keeps the same Reading Passage Card.

6. Partner B reads the passage card using the indicated emotion.

7. Partners take turns reading the same passage using four different Emotion Cards before choosing a new Reading Passage Card.

Blacklines

Reading Passage Cards
RallyRobin

Instructions: Copy for each pair.
Note: Copy on a different color of paper than the Emotion Cards.

Reading Passage Cards

One day as I was walking through the forest, I spotted something rather unusual. I wasn't quite sure what it was, so I decided to investigate.

Reading Passage Cards

Today my mom will drive me to my new school. We moved from out-of-state last week. Who will I meet? Will I make new friends? What will my teacher be like?

Reading Passage Cards

I sat in the stands at the football game waiting for the game between North High and Southwest to begin. My thoughts traveled back to the last game they played.

Reading Passage Cards

I just zipped up my bulging suitcase. I hear my mom and dad calling for me to come downstairs, so they can load the van. I look around the room to see if I have everything I'll need for the next two weeks.

Reading Passage Cards

I sat on the front row waiting my turn to perform my piano piece for the large crowd, which sat behind me. I had practiced my solo for many weeks and knew it well. I heard my name being called.

Reading Passage Cards

It was the middle of the third quarter of the basketball game with our rival team, the Falcons. The score was tied at 64-64. My heart was beating as loud as the drum in the band.

Emotion Cards
RallyRobin

Instructions: Copy for each pair.
Note: Copy on a different color of paper than the Reading Passage Cards.

Emotion Cards	Emotion Cards
fearful	**miserable**
Emotion Cards	Emotion Cards
excited	**joyful**
Emotion Cards	Emotion Cards
angry	**hurt**
Emotion Cards	Emotion Cards
lonely	**cheery**

Emotion Cards
RallyRobin

Instructions: Copy for each pair.
Note: Copy on a different color of paper than the Reading Passage Cards.

Emotion Cards	Emotion Cards
tearful	**glad**
unsure	**tired**
amused	**uncomfortable**
upset	**scared**

Emotion Cards
RallyRobin

Instructions: Copy for each pair.
Note: Copy on a different color of paper than the Reading Passage Cards.

Emotion Cards	Emotion Cards
confused	**depressed**
frustrated	**content**
worried	**pleased**
bored	**overwhelmed**

Balanced Literacy

Comprehension ◯

Word Study ◯

Fluency ◯

Writing ✓

Writing

Writing

Authors use four main text types to convey meaning in print:

- **Narrative**—to entertain
- **Expository**—to inform
- **Technical**—to tell how to...
- **Persuasive**—to convince

Expository writing is a great starting place for students. Children naturally write in expository form, informing us of what they know or are learning from their experiences. Many states are testing students' proficiency in comprehending expository text, which is often more challenging for students. Therefore, this section focuses on writing an expository piece with the goal of strengthening both expository reading and writing.

Writing and reading are reciprocal processes, each supporting the other. Understanding why and how authors use text features helps students apply these same organizational features in their own writing.

This writing section is organized in sequential lessons that will produce an expository piece of writing through a cooperative group learning process. The goal is for students to apply what they have learned through group work to their individual writing.

Note: The teacher should have his or her own ongoing piece of writing that is used for modeling in each lesson.

Table of Writing Resources

Page(s)	Resources	Balanced Literacy				
		Aloud	Shared	Guided	Independent	Literature Circles
388	Expository Writing Resource Descriptions					
389	Expository Writing Model	●	●	●	●	
390	Expository Writing Steps	●	●	●	●	
391	Six Trait Checklist for Expository Writing	●	●	●	●	

Table of Writing Activities

Page(s)	Activities	Blacklines	Balanced Literacy				
			Aloud	Shared	Guided	Independent	Literature Circles
394	Expository Writing Stages	• Teacher Resource Lesson Guide					
395	**Inside-Outside Circle Activity**						
395	Pre-Writing Circles	• Pre-Writing Question Cards	●		●		
397	**Jot Thoughts Activity**						
397	Brainstorming Ideas	• Brainstorming Mat	●			●	
399	**RoundTable Consensus Activity**						
399	Sorting Ideas	• Sorting Mat	●	●	●		
401	**Solo Activities**						
401	Paragraph Writing	• SAMPLE Topic Sentence Form • SAMPLE Detail Sentence Form • Topic Sentence Form • Detail Sentences Form	●			●	
406	**RoundRobin Activities**						
406	Improving Details	• Six Ways to Improve Details • Detail Improvement Form	●	●	●	●	
409	**CenterPiece Activities**						
409	Word Choice Practice	• Word Choice—Powerful Verbs • Word Choice—Powerful Verbs (Possible Answers) • Word Choice—Powerful Adjectives • Word Choice—Powerful Adjectives (Possible Answers) • Word Choice—Similes • Word Choice—Describing a Noun • Word Choice—Form	●	●	●	●	

Balanced Literacy • Third Grade • Skidmore & Graber
Kagan Publishing • 1 (800) 933-2667 • www.KaganOnline.com

Table of Writing Activities (continued)

Page(s)	Activities	Blacklines	Balanced Literacy				
			Aloud	Shared	Guided	Independent	Literature Circles
418	**RallyCoach Activity**						
418	Sentence Writing Practice	• Sentence Mechanics • Revising Sentences • Revising Sentences Form					
424	**Team Stand-N-Share Activity**						
424	Hooks and Endings	• Hook Examples • Ending Examples • Hook and Ending Form—Sample • Hook and Ending Form	●	●	●	●	
429	**Two-Partner Edit Activity**						
429	Six Trait Feedback	• Six Trait Checklist for Expository Writing			●		
430	**Mix-Pair-Share Activity**						
430	Sharing Final Drafts				●		

Writing
Resources

Expository Writing Resources

Writing Resource Descriptions

One key to scaffolding instruction is the inclusion of modeling. **The teacher should have his or her own ongoing piece of writing that is used for modeling in each lesson**. This permits the students to see the skill being used, creates a better understanding of what is expected, and allows for more effective application of the skill.

Expository Writing Model (p. 389)
The hook, fish, and tail graphics are visuals, that can be used to increase the students' understanding of the parts of an expository writing piece.
• **Hook** = beginning sentence(s) that engage the reader and make him or her want to continue reading
• **Fish (Mighty Middle)** = the topic sentences and supporting details, that provide the information and facts relating to the topic
• **Tail End** = the ending gives the writing natural closure

Expository Writing Steps (p. 390)
The organization of expository writing is necessary to move the reader through the text: hook, mighty middle, and ending. As you notice, the writer will start with the informational part of the piece first (mighty middle). Once the writer has organized his or her information, the teacher will use focus lessons to help students revise to produce a quality writing piece. The beginning hook comes next. The writer will create a hook that will draw the reader in and make him or her want to continue reading. Because the writer has already written the mighty middle and knows the information he or she is presenting to the reader, it will be easier for him or her to write an appropriate hook. The tail end comes last. The purpose of the ending is to bring the writing to a satisfying closure, tying up loose ends for the reader.

Six Trait Checklist for Expository Writing (p.391)
Ideas, organization, voice, word choice, sentence fluency, and conventions are six trait writing components used to evaluate the student's writing performance. In this section, a six trait checklist is provided to increase student awareness of qualities that make up each component. After students complete their writing, the students can evaluate their writing by placing an "X" on the line indicating the qualities used in their writing. This visual will help students realize which areas they need to work on for improvement. Once the students have experience self-evaluating and have a clear understanding of the characteristics that make up each trait, the teacher can move students from a checklist to a rubric.

Expository Writing Model

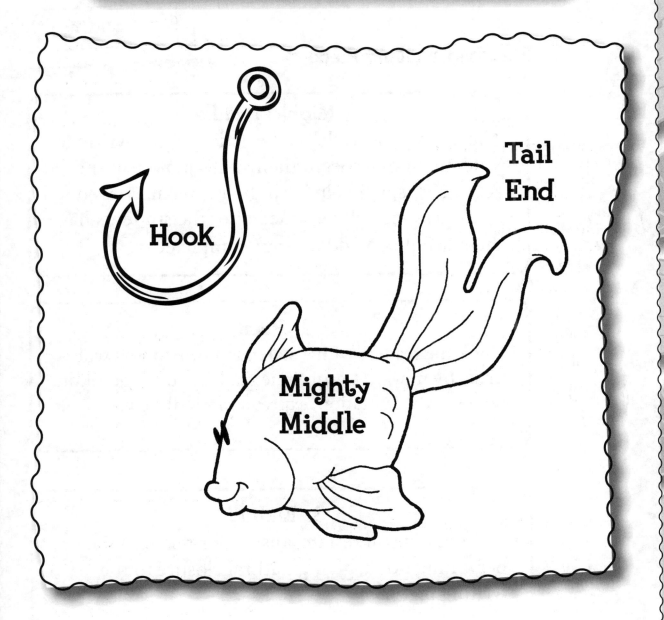

Hook

Tail End

Mighty Middle

Expository Writing Steps

Finished Writing Piece

1. Mighty Middle

- The "Mighty Middle" is the action of the writing.
- Students should begin their writing piece at the action. This will help keep their topic narrowed.
- Focus lessons will be added after the students have their "Mighty Middle" draft completed.

2. Hook

- Hook the readers with a statement or two that will make them want to continue reading: use a question, bold words, quotation, expression, riddle, etc.

3. Ending

- The ending will restate, answer, or relate to the beginning hook, giving natural closure to the writing piece.

Six Trait Checklist for Expository Writing

Name_____ **Date**_____

Instructions: The teacher determines how many of the six traits to evaluate. The student and/or teacher can evaluate a piece of writing by placing an 'X' on each line indicating the skill(s) being used to strengthen each trait. Copy for each student.

Ideas

___ My writing is focused and sticks to the topic.

___ My writing has a purpose: explain/inform.

___ My writing uses supporting details.

___ My writing lets the reader picture (visualize) what is happening.

___ My writing gives enough information to make it interesting. It tells things that not everyone knows.

Organization

___ My writing has a strong beginning hook that makes the reader want to continue.

___ My writing has a focused middle that sticks to the main idea.

___ My writing uses supporting details at the right places.

___ My writing has an ending that brings natural closure.

___ My writing is easy to follow.

Voice

___ My writing sounds like me. It does not sound like it is copied from a book.

___ My writing uses words that show my feelings.

___ My writing shows that I care about the topic.

___ My writing is appropriate for my audience.

___ My writing answers questions that readers might have.

Word Choice

___ My writing uses new words.

___ My writing uses strong verbs and specific nouns.

___ My writing uses supporting details.

___ My writing does not repeat the same words too many times.

___ My writing uses literary devices: comparison, simile, dialogue, humor, suspense, onomatopoeia, _____ (circle ones used).

Sentence Fluency

___ My writing uses sentences that are easy to read aloud.

___ My writing has some sentences that can be read expressively.

___ My writing uses sentences that begin in different ways.

___ My writing uses both long and short sentences.

___ My writing sounds the way I talk.

Conventions

___ My writing uses spaces between words.

___ My writing uses capital letters correctly.

___ My writing uses end marks correctly.

___ My writing has been checked for spelling (or my best try at spelling).

___ My writing starts a new paragraph when new information is presented.

Writing Activities

Expository Writing Stages

The following writing activities are sequenced to take students through the stages of writing an expository piece. Some of the activities are short and you can do multiple activities in one day. Other will take longer. There are also practice activities and forms integrated in this section to help students develop their expository writing skills. Below is an overview of the stages of writing and the activities included.

Prewriting (pp. 395–400)
- **Prewriting Circles**—Students ask partners prewriting questions to focus them on their writing topic.
- **Brainstorming Ideas**—Students brainstorm ideas related to their writing topic.
- **Sorting Ideas**—Students sort ideas into categories that will be developed into complete sentences.

Writing (p. 401-405)
- **Paragraph Writing**—Students develop their ideas into a topic sentence and supporting detail sentences.

Editing & Rewriting (pp. 406–428)
- **Improving Details**—Students learn six ways to improve their detail sentences and then work to improve their own detail sentences.
- **Word Choice Practice**—Students practice word choice and then work to improve the word choice in their expository writing.
- **Sentence Writing Practice**—Students practice rewriting sentences for mechanics and fluency.
- **Hooks and Endings**—Students write beginning hooks and endings to their expository writing pieces.

Peer Feedback (p. 429)
- **Six Trait Feedback**—Students get feedback from peers, focusing on the six traits.

Sharing (p. 430)
- **Sharing Final Drafts**—Students share their final drafts with peers as an audience.

Prewriting Circles

The amount of writing that students produce is in proportion to the amount of talking and processing that they get to do before they write. In this activity, students form two concentric circles so that pairs face each other. Using the questions provided, students ask their partner a question. The circles rotate multiple times so students share with multiple partners. This activity helps students focus on their topic, expand their writing ideas, and write in complete sentences.

STRUCTURE
Inside-Outside Circle

Activity Steps

1 Students are given time to choose a topic and read about their topic.

2 Students form pairs and each student is given one Prewriting Question Card.

3 One student from each pair moves to form one large circle.

4 Remaining students find and face their partners. (The class now stands in two concentric circles.)

5 The Inside Circle students ask the Outside Circle students the question on their question card. The Outside Circle students respond.

6 Partners switch roles: Outside Circle students ask the questions and Inside Circle students respond.

7 Students trade cards, then the Inside Circle students rotate clockwise to face a new partner to ask and answer a new prewriting question.

Blackline

Prewriting Question Cards
Inside-Outside Circle

Instructions: Make enough copies of this blackline so that each student has one card. Cut out the question cards and give each student one card. Students use cards to ask partners prewriting questions during Inside-Outside Circle.

Prewriting Questions What topic are you planning to write about?	**Prewriting Questions** What do you already Know about this topic?	**Prewriting Questions** What questions do you still have about this topic?
Prewriting Questions What is the most important idea to get across to your readers?	**Prewriting Questions** Where could you find more information about this topic?	**Prewriting Questions** What will readers find interesting about this topic?
Prewriting Questions What does this topic remind you of?	**Prewriting Questions** If you could add a photograph to your writing about this topic, what would it be?	**Prewriting Questions** What information about this topic will you not include in your writing?
Prewriting Questions How can you present the topic so that it is not boring to read?	**Prewriting Questions** What words do you want to include in your writing about this topic?	**Prewriting Questions** What would be a good title for your writing? Why?

Brainstorming Ideas

Students brainstorm in teams using Jot Thoughts. They write one word, phrase, or sentence about their topic, read it aloud to the team, then place the idea on a mat with the topic in the center of the table. This process frees students' minds to generate information without worrying about organization. Creative and varied responses are encouraged as students read their ideas aloud to spark additional ideas.

Activity Steps

STRUCTURE
Jot Thoughts

1. Each team gets a Brainstorming Mat. They write the writing topic in the center of the mat. Students each have sticky notes and a pen.

2. Students write the ideas that come to mind on the sticky note, and place it on the mat. They announce their idea to the team.

3. The team tries to completely cover the mat with ideas about the topic.

Sample Brainstorming Mat.

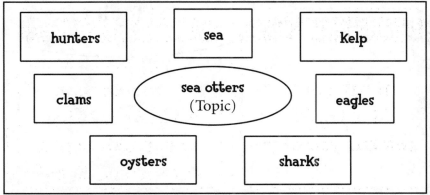

Blackline

Brainstorming Mat
Jot Thoughts

Instructions: Write your writing topic in the center of this mat. As a team, brainstorm ideas relating to the topic on sticky notes and place them on the mat. Announce your idea to teammates as you place it on the mat. (Make one copy per team.)

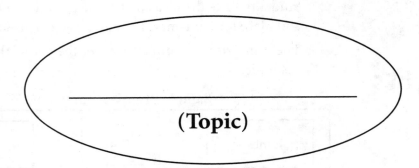

(Topic)

Sorting Ideas

After students have generated numerous ideas relating to the topic, they use RoundTable Consensus to physically sort the ideas into categories on a sorting mat. The concrete aids help students organize expository information into groups that are later developed into paragraphs.

Activity Steps

STRUCTURE

RoundTable Consensus

1. Each team gets a Sorting Mat and their ideas generated from the previous activity.

2. The first student selects a sticky note, places the note on the Sorting Mat, and announces the possible category or reason for sorting.

3. Teammates show agreement or lack of agreement with thumbs up or thumbs down.

4. If there is agreement, the team celebrates and the next student places the next idea on the sorting mat. If there is not consensus, students discuss the idea until they reach agreement.

5. When all items are sorted, students take turns labeling each category, checking for consensus before writing.

Sample Sorting Mat.

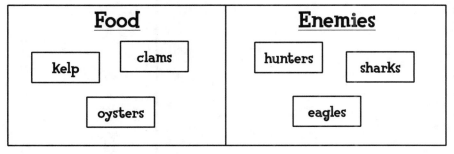

Blackline

Sorting Mat
RoundTable Consensus

Instructions: Students take turns sorting ideas into like categories. Once all ideas are sorted, students label categories. Make one copy per team.

Paragraph Writing

Now that students have their ideas sorted into categories, they are ready to develop each category into a paragraph. To do this, they independently write the topic sentence of a paragraph, followed by supporting detail sentences.

Activity Steps

STRUCTURE

Solo

1. Copy the Topic Sentence Form on light-colored paper and the Detail Sentences Form on a different light-colored paper. Give both sheets to each student.

2. Using the Sample Topic Sentence Form, model for students how to fill out their Topic Sentence Forms.

3. Students complete their Topic Sentence Form by writing the 1) Topic 2) Question 3) Topic Sentence. Then, they cut out the topic sentence for later use.

4. Next, model for students how to turn an idea into a complete written sentence using the Sample Detail Sentences Form.

5. Students select three individual sticky notes and write them as three complete detail sentences on the form.

6. Students cut the three detail sentences apart and select their favorite sequence. Then, they tape the sentences together in the preferred sequence, and tape the topic sentence on top.

Blacklines

SAMPLE
Topic Sentence Form

Instructions: Use this form to model how to develop a topic sentence.

Topic

Enemies

Question

Who are the sea otter's enemies?

Topic Sentence

The sea otter needs to watch out for several enemies.

SAMPLE
Detail Sentences Form

Instructions: Use this form to model how to develop detail sentences.

 # 1 Sharks and whales are dangerous enemies of sea otters. Great white sharks eat 10-20% of sea otters. They think otters are sea lions, their favorite food. They attack and grab the otters from underwater.

 # 2 Eagles are a threat to sea otter pups. When the mother otter dives for food, the pup is left alone and can be picked up by an eagle.

 # 3 Hunters killed sea otters for their thick, soft fur. This fur was very special because it is thicker than any other mammal fur. So many otters were killed for fur to make clothes that almost all of them were gone. Today, hunting sea otters is against the law.

Topic Sentence Form

Instructions: Write your paragraph topic in the box below. Then write the topic as a question. Then write the question as a topic sentence. Cut out your topic sentence. (Make one copy per student.)

Topic

Question

Topic Sentence

Detail Sentences Form

Instructions: Write a detail sentence in each box below. Cut them out, then sequence them in the best order. Number the sentences in order from 1–3. Tape them together in the sequence you like. Then, tape your Topic Sentence (page 404) on top. (Make one copy per student.)

#_____ _____

_____

_____

_____

_____

#_____ _____

_____

_____

_____

_____

#_____ _____

_____

_____

_____

_____

Improving Details

Students have each written a paragraph about the topic. Now, their task is to improve their paragraphs by adding details to text. The teacher models how to improve details. Students work independently to add details and share their improvements with teammates.

Activity Steps

1. Using the Six Ways to Improve Details form, share with students the various ways they can improve their writing.

2. Students select one detail sentence they have written. They select which of the six methods they plan to use to improve the information. The Detail Improvement Form on page 408 is used to record the improvements.

3. Students then share the new and improved sentence with teammates.

4. Teammates hold up 1–6 fingers to guess which idea for improvement their teammate used. The student informs the team which method he or she used and congratulates students who guessed correctly.

5. They repeat the process for the other two sentences, choosing different ways to improve their other sentences.

STRUCTURE

RoundRobin

Blacklines

Six Ways to Improve Details

Instructions: Use this form to share with students six ways to write and improve detail sentences.

Comparison

Frogs and toads are alike in many ways.

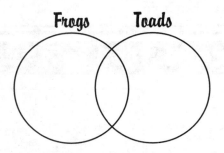

Personal Experience

When I was visiting San Francisco Bay, I was able to watch a sea otter lay on its back, hold its food with its front paws, and use a stone to crack open a clam.

Number Word

There are more than 350 types of sharks found all around the world.

Description

Sharks have rows of razor sharp teeth, excellent hearing, and sharp eyes that help them see in the dim, deep water.

Text Feature

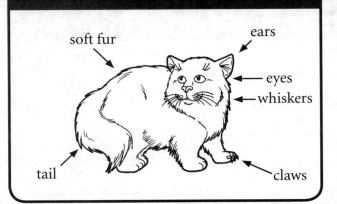

soft fur

ears

eyes

whiskers

tail

claws

Specific Name or Example

The killer whale, or orca, is referred to as the wolf of the sea because it travels in a pack to hunt for food.

Detail Improvement Form

Instructions: Rewrite your three detail sentences below. For each sentence, pick one of the 6 ideas for improvement. Write the idea for improvement number in the circle. If needed, use the box to add text features. Share one sentence at a time with teammates and see if they can pick which idea for improvement you used.

6 Ways to Improve My Sentences

1. Comparison
2. Personal Experience
3. Number Word
4. Description
5. Text Feature (graph, diagram, chart, definition, picture)
6. Specific Name or Example

Detail Sentence #1

Detail Sentence #2

Detail Sentence #3

Word Choice Practice

Students continue to improve their writing by adding descriptive language to engage the reader. Students brainstorm and share word choice ideas. Blacklines are included to practice verb choice, adjective choice, similes, and describing nouns.

Activity Steps

STRUCTURE

CenterPiece

1. Each team is given five items, focusing on the same word choice skill. For example, to practice verb choice, each team is given five verb cards (run, eat, look, talk, walk).

2. Students each get one card and one card is placed in the center of the team table (the centerpiece).

3. Students brainstorm one alternate word choice for their word card, write the new word on the card, and exchange their card with the centerpiece. For example, for the word *eat*, examples may include *snarf, munch, shoe, etc.*

4. Students continue brainstorming and trading their papers with the centerpiece until time is up or until they can't think of additional ideas.

5. Share additional word choices with students (blacklines provided).

6. After practicing word choice, students revise their paragraphs to improve word choice.

7. This process is repeated with other word choice topics (e.g., adjectives, similes).

Blacklines

Word Choice—Powerful Verbs
CenterPiece

Instructions: Cut out cards. Each teammate gets one card and one is the centerpiece. Brainstorm one powerful verb, write it on your card, and then trade your card with the centerpiece. Continue brainstorming, writing, and trading to generate many alternatives for each word.

run

eat

look

talk

walk

Word Choice—Powerful Verbs

Possible Answers

Instructions: Share these possible word choices with students after they generate their own.

run

hurry	scurry	gallop	whiz
bolt	speed	sprint	zoom
race	dash	trot	
dart	jog	rush	

eat

devour	feast	smack
picnic	feed	munch
graze	gobble	lick
dine	slurp	grind

look

glare	gaze	observe	search
stare	glance	seek	glimpse
spot	see	examine	notice
watch	spy	gawk	sight

talk

speak	jabber	whisper	remark	state	reply
warn	mutter	quarrel	tell	respond	
murmur	babble	discuss	call	shout	
argue	chat	squeak	report	demand	

walk

stroll	stray	saunter	leap	parade
march	strut	hop	stagger	amble
trudge	stride	skip	shuffle	
hike	roam	lumber	travel	

Word Choice—Powerful Adjectives
CenterPiece

Instructions: Cut out cards. Each teammate gets one card and one is the centerpiece. Brainstorm one powerful adjective, write it on your card, and then trade your card with the centerpiece. Continue brainstorming, writing, and trading to generate many alternatives for each word.

little

big

happy

smart

good

Word Choice—Powerful Adjectives
Possible Answers

Instructions: Share these possible word choices with students after they generate their own.

little

teeny	small	microscopic
compact	tiny	miniature
petite	slight	
wee	minute	

big

towering	large	gigantic
tremendous	giant	immense
huge	great	mammoth
massive	colossal	enormous

happy

glad	thrilled	merry	pleased
delighted	elated	jubilant	
joyful	cheerful	contented	
jolly	jovial	cheery	

smart

witty	intelligent	wise
brilliant	clever	gifted
bright	sharp	brainy
sharp	knowledgeable	

good

great	marvelous	wonderful
amazing	superb	terrific
pleasant	delightful	superior
splendid	grand	excellent

Word Choice — Similes
CenterPiece

Instructions: Cut out cards. Each teammate gets one card and one is the centerpiece. Brainstorm one simile, write it on your card, and then trade your card with the centerpiece. Continue brainstorming, writing, and trading to generate as many similes as you can.

slow as ...

cold as ...

sweet as ...

big as ...

hot as ...

Word Choice — Similes
CenterPiece

Instructions: Cut out cards. Each teammate gets one card and one is the centerpiece. Brainstorm one simile, write it on your card, and then trade your card with the centerpiece. Continue brainstorming, writing, and trading to generate as many similes as you can.

quick like ...

loud as ...

soft like ...

hairy as ...

sharp as ...

Word Choice—Describing a Noun
CenterPiece

Instructions: Cut out cards. Each teammate gets one card and one is the centerpiece. Brainstorm one adjective to describe the noun, write it on your card, and then trade your card with the centerpiece. Continue brainstorming, writing, and trading to generate as many adjectives as you can.

monkey

truck

baby

tree

dolphin

Balanced Literacy • Third Grade • Skidmore & Graber
Kagan Publishing • 1 (800) 933-2667 • www.KaganOnline.com

Word Choice—Form
CenterPiece

Instructions: Use this form to create more word choice activities. Write the word in the blank provided. Students brainstorm alternatives on the card.

Activity

Sentence Writing Practice

Students practice rewriting sentences in pairs. Blacklines are provided to practice mechanics, substituting words, adding words, deleting words, and using descriptive language. A form is provided for the teacher to create additional practice sentences.

Activity Steps

1 Each pair receives a set of sentence strips. They place the sentence strips facedown between them.

2 Partner A turns over the first sentence strip and reads it aloud. He or she then describes how he or she is going to rewrite the sentence.

3 Partner B is the coach. The coach makes suggestions or approves the rewriting plan.

4 Partner A rewrites the sentence.

5 Partners switch roles for each sentence strip so they both get practice rewriting and offering suggestions.

6 After practicing rewriting sentences, students revisit their writing again to see if they can improve it with new skills.

STRUCTURE
RallyCoach

Blacklines

Sentence Mechanics
RallyCoach

Instructions: Cut out sentence strips. Place them facedown between you and your partner. Partner A turns over the first one, reads it, and describes how to rewrite the sentence. Partner B offers suggestions or agrees. Partner A then rewrites the sentence. Switch roles for each sentence strip.

Sentence Mechanics

1. we found our cat in new york city

Sentence Mechanics

2. if I had a new pet, I would name it fluffy

Sentence Mechanics

3. the salesperson said she was busy until october

Sentence Mechanics

4. is french toast mike's favorite breakfast food

Sentence Mechanics

5. how fast did jane run in the race on monday

Sentence Mechanics

6. john wore a tall hat on president's day

Sentence Mechanics

7. did you play a trick on april fool's day

Sentence Mechanics
RallyCoach

Instructions: Cut out sentence strips. Place them facedown between you and your partner. Partner A turns over the first one, reads it, and describes how to rewrite the sentence. Partner B offers suggestions or agrees. Partner A then rewrites the sentence. Switch roles for each sentence strip.

Sentence Mechanics

8. the roses were in bloom on the fourth of july

Sentence Mechanics

9. mary will go to dr rogers for a checkup

Sentence Mechanics

10. my best friend was mrs anna gomez

Sentence Mechanics

11. we went to florida on vacation in june

Sentence Mechanics

12. they will take the bus to denver on tuesday

Sentence Mechanics

13. our new address is 233 south pine street

Sentence Mechanics

14. sue, pat, and randy live in seattle washington

Revising Sentences
(Substitute, Add, or Delete Words for More Descriptive Writing)

RallyCoach

Instructions: Cut out sentence strips. Place them facedown between you and your partner. Partner A turns over the first one, reads it, and describes how to rewrite the sentence. Partner B offers suggestions or agrees. Partner A then rewrites the sentence. Switch roles for each sentence strip.

Revising Sentences

1. The dog ran to the house.

Revising Sentences

2. Sally saw a bird flying fast.

Revising Sentences

3. A tree moved in the wind.

Revising Sentences

4. Monkeys are very nice to see.

Revising Sentences

5. I took the paper off my present.

Revising Sentences

6. Tomorrow we will go.

Revising Sentences

7. John got a fish on his pole.

Revising Sentences
(Substitute, Add, or Delete Words for More Descriptive Writing)
RallyCoach

Instructions: Cut out sentence strips. Place them facedown between you and your partner. Partner A turns over the first one, reads it, and describes how to rewrite the sentence. Partner B offers suggestions or agrees. Partner A then rewrites the sentence. Switch roles for each sentence strip.

Revising Sentences

8. It was very, very, very, very cold.

Revising Sentences

9. We put the cake on the table.

Revising Sentences

10. Jane bought milk and eggs and bread.

Revising Sentences

11. The candle was burning.

Revising Sentences

12. Students stood in the hall.

Revising Sentences

13. When the wind came papers moved.

Revising Sentences

14. Dave read good books.

Balanced Literacy • Third Grade • Skidmore & Graber
Kagan Publishing • 1 (800) 933-2667 • www.KaganOnline.com

Revising Sentences Form

Instructions: Use this blackline to create your own sentence strips for partners to practice revising.

Revising Sentences

Revising Sentences

Revising Sentences

Revising Sentences

Revising Sentences

Revising Sentences

Revising Sentences

Hooks and Endings

Students learn to write paragraph openers to "hook" the reader and endings to give the writing a natural closure. Teams investigate other writing samples and share what hooks and endings writers use.

Activity Steps

1. Students look through expository magazines, such as *National Geographic Kids* and *Ranger Rick*, noticing different ways authors begin articles.

2. Using RoundTable, the team generates a list of hooks.

3. After teams have enough time to collect multiple ideas, the teacher asks the class to stand.

4. The teacher calls on a standing student.

5. The selected student states one idea from the team list.

6. The student in each team who is holding the team list either adds the item to the list, or if it is already listed, checks it off. The teacher also makes a master list of student ideas.

7. Teammates pass their team list one teammate clockwise.

8. Teams sit when all their items are shared. While seated they add each new item as it is stated using RoundTable. When all teams are seated, Team Stand-N-Share is complete.

9. The teacher may use the Hook Examples blackline to share additional hook ideas.

10. Students repeat the process examining and sharing ending ideas.

11. Finally, students use the Hook & Ending Form to write a new hook and ending for their paper.

STRUCTURE
Team Stand-N-Share

Blacklines

Hook Examples

Instructions: Use this form to share effective writing hooks with students.

● **Question**

What mammal has over half a million hairs per square inch?

● **Riddle**

I am a very intelligent mammal. I know how to use a rock to crack open clams to eat? WHAT AM I?

● **Exclamation**

WOW! What a SMART idea! I never thought kelp could be used as an anchor, but a sea otter has it all figured out. It wraps itself up in kelp while taking a nap, so that it doesn't float away.

● **Onomatopoeia**

Z-z-z-z-z-z!
Sh-sh-sh! The sea otter is fast asleep on its back with its paws covering its eyes while floating in the sea.

● **Alliteration**

I saw carnivores crunching on crustaceans, crabs, and cracked clams.

● **Exaggeration**

As I stepped out on the rocky shore, I saw sleek, furry bodies gliding as fast as torpedoes through the water.

● **Description**

Sea otters are furry, sleek marine mammals that live along rocky Pacific Ocean coasts.

Ending Examples

Instructions: Use this form to share effective writing endings with students.

● **Answer to Beginning Question**

With over half a million hairs per square inch, the sea otter definitely does have the densest fur of any mammal.

● **Reference Back to Riddle**

So after reading all about this special animal, you have probably guessed the answer to my riddle. The SEA OTTER is the smart mammal that figures out how to crack open a clam with a rock while floating on its back.

● **Generalization**

Sea otters are fascinating marine mammals.

● **Personal Comment**

I have learned that sea otters are amazing and very interesting animals. I now know why they are sometimes called, "Clowns of the Kelp Beds."

● **Restatement of Main Idea**

After reading about sea otters, you can see why it is important that laws continue to protect them from hunters.

● **Challenge to the Reader**

Find out more sea otter facts for yourself by searching the Web. I know you'll find adorable photographs that will probably put sea otters on the top of your favorite animal list.

 Balanced Literacy • Third Grade • Skidmore & Graber
Kagan Publishing • 1 (800) 933-2667 • www.KaganOnline.com

Hook & Ending Form— Sample

Instructions: Use this form to write a new hook and ending.

Type of Hook _Exclamation_

Hook
Look! A sea otter is taking a nap on his back while floating in a bed of kelp.

Middle

Type of Ending _Challenge to the reader, reference to hook._

Ending
Now, remember to be extra quiet! The sea otter is wrapping up in his bed of kelp for a long, relaxing nap.

Hook & Ending Form

Instructions: Use this form to write a new hook and ending.

Type of Hook _____

Hook

↓

Middle

↓

Type of Ending _____

Ending

Six Trait Feedback

Students share their writing with peers and receive feedback on six specific traits of their writing.

STRUCTURE

Two-Partner Edit

Activity Steps

1. Students complete a polished draft.

2. Students stand up, put a hand up, and pair up with a classmate.

3. The pair sits down at a table, each with their Six Trait Checklist (page 391).

4. Partner A reads his or her writing.

5. Partner B provides feedback on one of the six traits by reading each statement under the trait, discussing it, and putting a plus or minus by the statement.

6. Students switch roles and Partner A provides feedback to partner B.

7. Students thank each other and then pair up with another partner to examine the next trait. The process continues for six pairings, each focusing on a different trait.

8. After receiving feedback, students write a final draft.

Blacklines

Activity

Sharing Final Drafts

Students practice rewriting sentences in pairs. Blacklines are provided to practice mechanics, substituting words, adding words, deleting words, and using descriptive language. A form is provided for the teacher to create additional practice sentences.

Activity Steps

1. Each student takes his or her final draft, stands up, puts a hand up, and mixes in the classroom.
2. The teacher calls, "Pair."
3. Students pair up with the person closest to them, who is not from their team, and give a high five.
4. Students take turns sharing their expository writing pieces by reading them to their partners using RallyRobin. Students provide feedback to their partners. The feedback can be:
   - Open-ended reactions
   - Praise
   - Response to a provided gambit: "From your writing, I learned…"
   - Copycat gambit: Students repeat after the teacher a flattering phrase such as "Your expository writing was well written and tremendously informative!"
5. Students can do multiple rounds of peer sharing.

STRUCTURE
Mix-Pair-Share

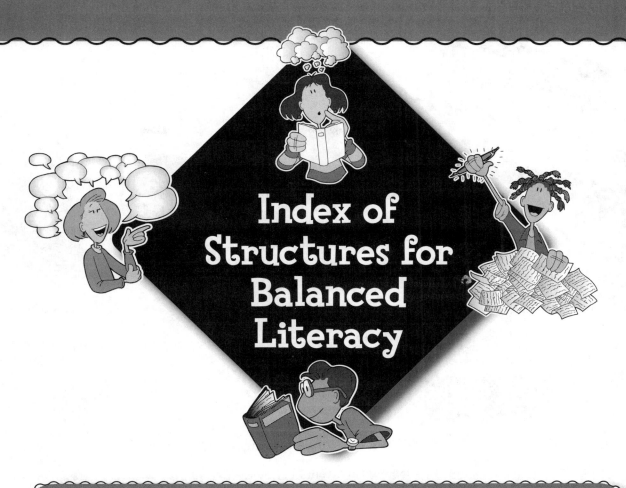

Index of Structures for Balanced Literacy

CenterPiece

Students brainstorm ideas, always trading their paper with the centerpiece.

Setup

• *Five pieces of paper per teams of four (one per person and one in the center)*

Steps

1 Teacher assigns a brainstorming topic.

2 Students generate items. They write one idea at a time and trade their paper with the one in the center.

3 Students continue brainstorming items, each time trading their paper with the centerpiece.

CenterPiece Activities and Blacklines

Fan-N-Pick

Students play a card game to respond to questions.

Setup

• *Each team receives a set of question cards.*

Steps

1 Student #1 holds question cards in a fan and says, "Pick a card, any card!"

2 Student #2 picks a card, reads the question aloud and allows five seconds of Think Time.

3 Student #3 answers the question.

4 Student #4 responds to the answer:
• For right or wrong answers, Student #4 checks and then either praises or tutors.
• For higher-level thinking questions that have no right or wrong answer, Student #4 does not check for correctness, but praises and paraphrases the thinking that went into the answer.

5 Students rotate roles, one person clockwise for each new round.

Fan-N-Pick Activities and Blacklines

Find My Rule

Students induce a rule from examples provided by the teacher.

mean
meat

rate
art

Steps

1. Teacher places one item in each area of the category frame.

2. Teacher asks, "What is my rule for placing items?" and provides think time.

3. Students RallyRobin with their shoulder partners to generate possible rules the teacher is using.

4. Teacher places two more objects in the category frame.

5. Teacher again says, "What is my rule?" and provides think time.

6. Students RallyRobin with their face partners to generate possible rules.

7. Teacher places more objects in the category frame, each time having teams discuss possible rules.

8. Teacher says, "Don't tell me your rule, name an item that fits in each category," and calls a number. Students with that number stand to share their items. The teacher confirms correct answers.

9. When most students seem to know the rule, the teacher calls on one student to verbalize the rule for the class.

10. Teacher confirms the rule.

11. Teacher presents new items one at a time, each time calling for students to hold up fingers indicating the category for the item.

12. Teacher congratulates the class.

Find My Rule Activities and Blacklines

Find Someone Who

Students mix about the room, finding others who help them learn content or skills.

Setup

• *The teacher prepares a worksheet or questions for students.*

Steps

1. Students mix in the class, keeping a hand raised until they find a new partner that is not a teammate.

2. In pairs, Partner A asks a question from the worksheet; Partner B responds. Partner A records the answer on his or her own worksheet.

3. Partner B checks and initials the answer.

4. Partner B asks a question. Partner A responds. Partner B records the answer on his or her own worksheet.

5. Partner A checks and initials the answer.

6. Partners shake hands, part, and raise a hand again as they search for a new partner.

7. Students repeat Steps 1–6 until their worksheets are complete.

8. When their worksheets are completed, students sit down; seated students may be approached by others as a resource.

9. In teams, students compare answers; if there is disagreement or uncertainty, they raise four hands to ask a team question.

Find Someone Who Activities and Blacklines

Inside-Outside Circle

In concentric circles, students rotate to face new partners and answer questions.

Setup

• *The teacher prepares questions or question cards for students. Students form pairs.*

Steps

1. One student from each pair moves to form one large circle in the class.

2. Remaining students find and face their partners. (The class now stands in two concentric circles.)

3. Inside circle students ask a question from their question card; outside circle students answer. Inside circle students praise or coach. (Alternative: The teacher asks a question and indicates inside person or outside person to share with their partner).

4. Partners switch roles.

5. Partners trade question cards.

6. Inside circle students rotate clockwise to a new partner. (The teacher may call rotation numbers: Rotate Three Ahead. The class may do a choral count as they rotate.

Note: When played with cards, Steps 3–6 become Quiz-Quiz-Trade.

Inside-Outside Circle Activity and Blacklines

Jot Thoughts

Teammates cover the table with ideas on slips of paper.

Steps

1. The teacher names a topic and sets a time limit.

2. Students announce and write as many ideas as they can in the allotted time, one idea per slip of paper.

3. Students attempt to cover the table with ideas (no slips are to overlap).

Jot Thoughts Activities and Blacklines

Listen-Sketch-Draft

Students sketch content chunk by chunk, create and compare main idea statements, and finally draft a summary statement.

Steps

1. Students listen while teacher presents the first chunk of information.

2. Teacher stops presenting and calls for each student to sketch the most important details.

3. Students share sketches using:
   • RoundRobin
   • Timed Pair Share

4. Students draft a main idea statement, based on the information shared in Step 1. While students draft their main ideas, teacher circulates and monitors.

5. The process is repeated for the next chunk.

6. When all chunks have been presented, students draft a summary statement.

7. Students compare their summaries with a partner or teammates praising ideas.

Listen-Sketch-Draft Activity and Blacklines

Mix-Pair-Share

Students pair with classmates to discuss questions posed by the teacher.

Setup

• Teacher prepares discussion questions to ask students.

Steps

1 Students silently mix around the room.

2 Teacher calls, "Pair."

3 Students pair up with the person closest them and give a high five. Students who haven't found a partner raise their hands to find each other.

4 Teacher asks a question and gives think time.

5 Students share with their partners using:
   • Timed Pair Share
   • RallyRobin
   • RallyCoach

Mix-Pair-Share Activity

Numbered Heads Together

Teammates work together to ensure all members understand; one is randomly selected to be held accountable.

Setup

• *Teacher prepares questions or problems to ask teams.*

Steps

1. Students number off.

2. Teacher poses a problem and gives think time. (Example: *Everyone think about how rainbows are formed.*)

3. Students privately write their answers.

4. Students lift up from their chairs to put their heads together, show answers, and discuss and teach.

5. Students sit down when everyone knows the answer or has something to share.

6. Teacher calls a number. The student with that number from each team answers simultaneously using:
   • Slate Share
   • Choral Practice
   • Finger Responses
   • Chalkboard Responses
   • Response Cards
   • Manipulatives

7. Teammates praise students who responded.

Numbered Heads Together Activities and Blacklines

Poems for Two Voices

Partners present a poem—recited at times by one partner, the other partner, or both.

Setup

• *The teacher prepares a poem with lines labeled A, B, or AB.*

Steps

1 Teacher explains and assigns students A and B roles.

2 Students read their labeled line, listening carefully to their partners to keep the flow.

Note: Students may progress through three stages:

1. Teacher provides poem and AB scripting.
2. Teacher provides poem and students provide AB scripting.
3. Students create or select poem and script it.

Poems for Two Voices Activities and Blacklines

Quiz-Quiz-Trade

Students quiz a partner, get quizzed by a partner, and then trade cards to repeat the process with a new partner.

Steps

1. Stand Up, Hand Up, Pair Up
2. Partner A quizzes.
3. Partner B answers.
4. Partner A praises or coaches.
5. Switch roles.
6. Partners trade cards.
7. Repeat Steps 1–6 a number of times.

*Text type, text structure, and figurative language **resources** are included in the Comprehension Resource Section pages.

Quiz-Quiz-Trade Activities and Blacklines

(continued on next page)

Structure

Quiz-Quiz-Trade (continued)

Students quiz a partner, get quizzed by a partner, and then trade cards to repeat the process with a new partner.

Quiz-Quiz-Trade Activities and Blacklines

Structure

RallyCoach

Partners take turns, one solving a problem while the other coaches.

Setup

- One set of high-consensus problems and one pencil per pair

Steps

1. Partner A solves the first problem.
2. Partner B watches and listens, checks, and praises.
3. Partner B solves the next problem.
4. Partner A watches and listens, checks, and praises.
5. Repeat starting at Step 1.

Note: RallyCoach may be used with worksheet problems, oral problems provided by the teacher, or manipulatives.

RallyCoach Activities and Blacklines

(continued on next page)

RallyCoach (continued)

Partners take turns, one solving a problem while the other coaches.

RallyCoach Activities and Blacklines

RallyRobin

In pairs, students alternate generating oral responses.

Steps

1. Teacher poses a problem to which there are multiple possible responses or solutions.

2. In pairs, students take turns stating responses or solutions.

RallyRobin Activities and Blacklines

RallyTable

In pairs, students alternate generating written responses or solving problems.

Setup

• *One paper and one pencil per pair*

Steps

1. Teacher poses a task to which there are multiple possible responses.

2. In pairs, students take turns passing the paper and pencil or pair project, each writing one answer or making a contribution.

   Variation: Simultaneous RallyTable. Students may each have their own piece of paper. Each writes at the same time and then trades at the same time.

RallyTable Activity and Blacklines

RoundRobin

In teams, students take turns responding orally.

Steps

1. Teacher assigns a topic or question with multiple possible answers.

2. In teams, students respond orally, each in turn taking about the same amount of time.

RoundRobin Activities and Blacklines

RoundTable

In teams, students take turns—generating written responses, solving problems, or making a contribution to the team project.

Setup

• *One piece of paper and one pencil per team*

Steps

1. Teacher provides a task to which there are multiple possible responses.

2. In teams, students take turns passing a paper and pencil or a team project, each writing one answer or making a contribution.

RoundTable Activities and Blacklines

RoundTable Consensus

In teams, students take turns answering questions or placing cards, checking for consensus each time.

Steps

1. Teacher provides or students generate question cards or manipulatives.

2. One student answers using manipulatives, if necessary.

3. The student checks for consensus.

4. The teammates show agreement or lack of agreement with thumbs up or down.

5. If there is agreement, the students celebrate and the next student responds. If not, teammates discuss the response until there is agreement and then they celebrate. If no agreement is reached, the card is set aside to be discussed later.

6. Play continues with the next student answering.

RoundTable Consensus Activities and Blacklines

Showdown

Students answer questions without help. Teams then share, check, and coach.

Setup

- *Teams each have a set of question cards stacked facedown in the center of the table.*

Steps

1. Teacher selects one student on each team to be the Showdown Captain for the first round.
2. Showdown Captain draws the top card and reads the question.
3. Working alone, all students write their answers.
4. When finished, teammates signal when they are ready.
5. The Showdown Captain calls, "Showdown."
6. Teammates show and state their answers.
7. Showdown Captain leads the checking.
8. If correct, the team celebrates; if not, teammates coach, then celebrate.
9. The person on the left of the Showdown Captain becomes the Showdown Captain for the next round.

Metacognitive and Text Structure resources are included in the Comprehension Resource Section on pages 10–13, 39–40.

Showdown Activities and Blacklines

Solo

Students write, read, draw, solve problems, or practice something on their own.

Steps

1 Teacher provides problem or activity for students.

2 Students engage in activity alone.

Solo Activities and Blacklines

Talking Chips

Students place a chip in the center of the table each time they talk.

Setup

• *Teams have talking chips (Maximum: two chips each)*

Steps

1. Teacher provides a discussion topic.

2. Any student begins the discussion, placing one of his or her chips in the center of the table.

3. Any student with a chip continues discussing, using his or her chip.

4. When all chips are used, teammates each collect their chips and continue the discussion using their talking chips.

Talking Chips Activity and Blacklines

Team Line-Ups

Students line up within their teams.

Setup

- *Teacher may prepare Line-Up cards or manipulatives for each team*

Steps

1. Teacher gives teammates a problem.
2. Within their teams, teammates line up in order of their answers.

Team Line-Ups Activity and Blacklines

Team Stand-N-Share

Teams stand to share their answers with the class.

Setup

• Teams need a list of items to share

Steps

1. All students stand near their teammates.

2. Teacher calls on a standing student.

3. Selected student states one idea from the team list.

4. The student in each team, who is holding the team list, either adds the item to the list, or if it is already listed, checks it off.

5. Students pass their team list one teammate clockwise.

6. Teams sit when all their items are shared. While seated they add each new item as it is stated using RoundTable. When all teams are seated, Team Stand-N-Share is complete.

Team Stand-N-Share Activity and Blacklines

Timed Pair Share

In pairs, students share with a partner for a predetermined time while the partner listens. Then partners switch roles.

Steps

1. The teacher announces a topic, states how long each student will share, and provides think time.

2. In pairs, Partner A shares; Partner B listens.

3. Partner B responds with a positive gambit.

4. Partners switch roles.

Hint: The teacher provides positive response gambits to use in Step 3:

Copycat response gambits
- *"Thanks for sharing!"*
- *"You are interesting to listen to!"*

Complete the sentence gambits
- *"One thing I learned listening to you was…."*
- *"I enjoyed listening to you because…."*
- *"Your most interesting idea was…."*

Timed Pair Share Activity and Blacklines

Traveling Heads Together

Students travel to new teams to share their team answer.

Setup

- *Teams have a list of items to share.*

Steps

1. Students number off in teams.
2. The teacher presents a problem and gives think time.
3. Teammates stand up and put their heads together to discuss and teach each other.
4. Students sit down when ready.
5. The teacher calls a student number and says how many teams to rotate ahead.
6. The student called rotates to the new team.
7. Students who rotated share their original team's answer with their new team.
8. If correct, teammates praise the visitor. If not, they correct and coach.

Alternative: Rather than rotating a specific number, One Stray may be used.

Traveling Heads Together Activities and Blacklines

Two-Partner Edit

After writing, students discuss and edit their work with a partner, then again with a second partner.

Steps

1. Students write alone on a topic.

2. When complete, students go to a predetermined area of the room to find another student who has finished writing.

3. Students pair up and find a place to sit, shoulder to shoulder.

4. In each pair, Student A reads his or her writing.

5. Students discuss the writing while Student A makes edits.

6. Students switch roles: Student B reads and makes edits.

7. Students thank their shoulder partner.

8. Students Stand Up, Hand Up, Pair Up.

9. With their new partner, students each read, discuss, and re-edit their papers.

Two-Partner Edit Activity and Blacklines

Notes

Notes

Notes

Notes

Notes